W9-APM-465

INFORMATION, ORGANIZATION, AND POWER

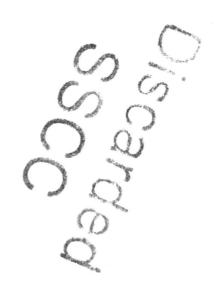

INFORMATION, ORGANIZATION, AND POWER

Effective Management in the Knowledge Society

Dale E. Zand

McGraw-Hill Book Company

New York   St. Louis   San Francisco   Auckland
Bogotá   Hamburg   Johannesburg   London   Madrid
Mexico   Montreal   New Delhi   Panama   Paris
São Paulo   Singapore   Sydney   Tokyo   Toronto

PERMISSIONS

Permission to adapt or reprint material from the following articles I have written is gratefully acknowledged.

"Managing the Knowledge Organization" in Peter F. Drucker, *Preparing Tomorrow's Business Leader Today,* © 1969, Prentice-Hall, Inc., pp. 112–136. Reprinted by permission: adapted for Chapters 1 and 2. "Trust and Managerial Problem Solving," © 1972, *Administrative Science Quarterly,* was adapted for Chapter 3. "Collateral Organization: A New Change Strategy," © 1974, *Journal of Applied Behavioral Science,* was adapted for Chapter 4. "Marketing Management Behavior," in *A New Measure of Responsibility for Marketing,* © 1969, American Marketing Association, was adapted for Chapter 5. "Change and the Effective Use of Management Science," © 1975, *Administrative Science Quarterly,* and "Improving the Implementation of OR/MS through the Lewin/Schein Model," in R. L. Schultz and D. P. Slevin, eds., *Implementing Operations Research/Management Science,* © 1975, American Elsevier Publishing Co. Inc., were sources for Chapter 6. Richard E. Sorensen, my coauthor for the last two articles, generously granted permission for adaptation from our joint publications. "Reviewing the Policy Process," © 1978 by the Regents of the University of California, reprinted from *California Management Review,* vol. 21, no. 1, pp. 35–46, by permission of the Regents: was modified for Chapter 7. "Managing the Board of Directors", © 1965, 1966, Ohio League of Savings Associations, was adapted for Chapter 8. "Management in Israel," © 1978, *Business Horizons,* was a source for Chapter 9. "Toward Understanding Behavior in an Industrial Society," in T. H. Bonaparte and J. E. Flaherty, eds., *Peter Drucker: Contributions to Business Enterprise,* © 1970, New York University Press, was adapted for Chapter 10.

Library of Congress Cataloging in Publication Data
Zand, Dale E.
    Information, organization, and power.

    Includes index.
    1. Communication in management. 2. Knowledge, Sociology of. 3. Management. I. Title.
HD30.3.Z36   658.4′038   80-21160
ISBN 0-07-072743-0

The editors for this book were William R. Newton and Esther Gelatt, the designer was Mark E. Safran, and the production supervisor was Sally Fliess. It was set in Garamond by Bi-Comp, Inc.

Printed and bound by The Murray Printing Company.

To my family:
Charlotte, Fern, Karen,
Mark, Jonathan, Matthew
For their love, patience, and understanding.

About the Author

ale E. Zand has been a consultant in policy analysis and organizational change to major organizations in the petroleum, banking, food, chemicals, and computer industries.

He has been Professor of Management at New York University since 1963 and was Chairman of the Management/Organizational Behavior Department of the Graduate School of Business from 1968 to 1978. He teaches in executive seminars conducted by major companies.

He received a Bachelor of Electrical Engineering from Cooper Union. He has an M.B.A. and a Ph.D. from New York University. He was a Ford Foundation Fellow at Harvard University.

He has presented papers to the Academy of Management, the Institute of Management Sciences, the American Psychological Association, and the International Congress of Applied Psychology. He has been chairman of the Organization Development Division and a member of the research committee of the Business Policy Division of the Academy of Management.

Contents

Preface

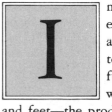I n our mass-consumption, industrialized society we have mastered the tasks of production and physical distribution. There will continue to be improvements in these activities, but the future of organizations in society resides less with the people who work with their hands and feet—the production workers—and more with the people who work with their heads—the managerial knowledge workers.

This book examines the process of management in a society driven by the search for and the application of knowledge. In a knowledge society, managers and staff specialists diligently seek and process knowledge. Their materials are ideas and opinions, assumptions and concepts, proposals and decisions. Their work with people concentrates on exchanging, extruding, and shaping knowledge. Their projections and conclusions direct and organize the repetitive production and marketing activities of the business.

Historically, some types of knowledge, such as finance, manufacturing, and engineering, have been considered more appropriate for men than for women. Knowledge, however, is blind to gender. As increasing numbers of women enter the labor force and the ranks of management, social conventions for associating knowledge with one or the other sex are vanishing. To avoid cumbersome language in this book, masculine pronouns, and such terms as "chairman" and "manpower," are used to refer to both men and women.

THE MEANING OF POWER

Power is shifting in organizations. The meaning of power is changing, and managers are walking a tightrope trying to balance the power of hierarchical position with the power of knowledge. A manager still has the right to give an order, as in the old production organization, but when his orders are knowledge deficient, he may lead the organization to serious loss or disrupt coordination with other units.

In a knowledge society, the manager's effective power is the product of his formal power multiplied by his knowledge competence. If he is near zero in either factor he will have little effective power.

KNOWLEDGE AND MANAGERIAL BEHAVIOR

This book analyzes the interplay between managerial behavior and the organization's growing dependence on knowledge. It looks at the effects of knowledge on organizations and their decision processes.

The book consists of three parts. The first part examines the characteristics of organizations in a knowledge society. It investigates the problems of finding knowledge and then converting it to useful products or services. If knowledge drives the organization, what strategies are there for getting it? What does it mean to manage a knowledge-centered organization where processing knowledge occurs in all activities and goes far beyond the traditional research laboratory? What are the characteristics of people who work with knowledge, and what demands do they place on managers? These are some of the issues addressed in the first two chapters.

Access to knowledge in an organization depends on how much managers trust each other. Trust differs from affection and amiability. It affects the quality of decisions by regulating the flow of information, receptivity to influence, and willingness to exercise self-control for a common goal. Chapter 3 discusses these effects and the factors that increase or decrease trust.

In addition to trust, however, a manager's beliefs about how to use his organization may determine his ability to discover problems and process relevant knowledge. Because many operating and policy situations are ill structured, managers must introduce new norms of behavior to supplement the formal organization with more effective ways of processing knowledge for making decisions. Chapter 4 explains the characteristics of a "collateral organization" and describes its application in two companies.

Part Two considers several crucial aspects of management in the context of a knowledge society. For example, marketing is an important, continuing source of knowledge, but marketing managers are invariably the center of much controversy. Is there something about the knowledge that marketers seek and how they process it that is different and therefore difficult for managers of other functions to understand? Why do nonmarketers often consider marketing management perplexing and irritating? For the marketer who aspires to top management, what are the implications of these fundamental differences in knowledge processing? These are the themes of Chapter 5.

In most organizations, staff groups are a repository of specialized knowledge and analytic abilities. If a staff does not have understanding and skill in inducing change in operating management, much of its knowledge and analytic potential are wasted. Chapter 7 discusses several approaches to transferring knowledge from staff to line operations. It introduces a framework for examining the process of change and identifies the characteristics of successful and unsuccessful staff change efforts.

Ultimately, management takes knowledge and shapes it into policy. The great-man theory of policy formulation says an organization should find a wise, rational prophet, appoint him chief executive, and follow his policies. The procedure theory says an organization should make policy formulation an extension of forecasting and financial budgeting. Both have merit, but for the modern, knowledge processing organization, they have crucial deficiencies. Chapter 7 presents a comprehensive, problem-solving approach and describes how it aids knowledge processing for policy decisions.

The last chapter in Part Two examines the board of directors, the figurative capstone of the organization. Although the board is at the top of the organization, its contribution is often enigmatic and its performance problematic. A knowledge society is increasingly unwilling to accept poorly managed boards: It cannot afford the economic and social costs. The theme of this chapter centers on what can be done to improve the management of the board, how it processes knowledge, and how it links to the organization.

Part Three, the concluding part of the book, steps back and looks at two underlying currents in management. One is the demand in every organization to manage stability and change. We are constantly confronted by the tensions created as each flows into the other. Fortunately, we have much knowledge about managing stability. The danger is to assume that stability will manage itself, or that it is too unimportant to manage, and then ignore the knowledge we have.

The second underlying current, and the final theme of the book, is the role of the individual—the industrial citizen—in a knowledge society. Organizations are key institutions, providing goods, services, and employment. They can be beneficial or detrimental. They can treat individuals as instruments to be used like any other tool to maximize output, or they can attempt to encourage wider use of our distinctly human abilities to think, to use knowledge, and to grow. The direction an organization takes depends on the guidance we—its citizens (managers, workers, consumers, and so on)—provide. The issues are complex, and the answers are not simple; but the choices are ours.

Dale E. Zand

Acknowledgments

anagement in the next 25 years will differ from what it has been in the past 25 years. Advances in knowledge assure that changes in management will occur. The fact that we are primarily knowledge-seeking and knowledge-using creatures will accelerate change and make it inevitable. In this book I examine management in the setting of a knowledge society and consider how the processing of knowledge increasingly affects how we manage.

Although I was not aware of it at the time, the intellectual seeds for this book were planted a little over 10 years ago when Peter Drucker asked me to talk about "Managing the Knowledge Organization" at a symposium celebrating the fiftieth anniversary of the New York University Graduate School of Business Administration. I thank him for the invitation and express my appreciation for the rich, provocative stimulus his writings have been to me.

Rensis Likert, Herbert Simon, and the late Douglas McGregor, among many notable contributors to this field, have also influenced the development of my thinking.

My faculty colleagues and the administration at New York University provided a climate conducive to investigating the issues and implications of management in a knowledge society.

Finally, I wish to record my deep appreciation to the many executives I have worked with over a period of more than 20 years. Confidentiality requires that they remain anonymous.

They discussed with me their interests and dilemmas, their aspirations and concerns as they sought to improve their organization's processing of knowledge. I observed their willingness to experiment in the face of resistance and their courage in accepting risks. Often they deserved greater recognition and rewards than they received.

PART 1

FINDING KNOWLEDGE

1. The Management of Knowledge

Management has been affected by one development in our culture that stands out above all others: We are becoming a knowledge society, and business enterprises are becoming knowledge-processing organizations.

A massive system of public education guides the knowledge development of more than 60 million children and adults. We employ more than 2 million educators in this country. Adult education, once considered a pastime, has become "continuing education"—a necessity for simply keeping up with the explosive growth of knowledge. Project "head start" reached back to the cradle, and the "job corps" and the "teacher corps" continued in hot educational pursuit of the "high school dropout." A comprehensive system of scholarships, student loans, and low-tuition public universities practically assures a college education and even graduate studies to every student with sufficient ability and motivation.

Although unheralded in the public press, business organizations have been a major stimulant of the quest for knowledge. Increasingly, they demand well-educated, knowledgeable new employees—in many firms a college education is a minimum condition for employment. Many firms provide tuition support to those who wish to continue their education; some firms give full-time scholarships to employees. Universities receive from businesses unrestricted donations as well as substantial grants for specific research projects. In addition, many large firms are directly engaged in disseminating and generating knowledge. For example, organizations like General Electric, General Motors, and IBM not only send managers and professional employees to university programs, they also maintain educational facilities and operate educational programs that rival the largest universities.

This evolution in the basic quality of our society portends significant changes for managers. We can get a glimpse of the magnitude of what lies ahead by reviewing some of the social and economic effects of earlier transitions.

Subtle changes with dramatic consequences

Three hundred years ago we were an agricultural society. People worked in family units that were physically and socially self-contained. Life's major activity was to sow and harvest the fruits of the soil. Markets were primitive, and management as we know it today did not exist—indeed, could not exist.

One hundred fifty years ago we began the transition to an industrial capital society. Isolated industrial organizations erupted on the social landscape. In time they became key institutions. They mobilized great masses of people, contributed to the economic well-being of citizens far beyond the factory gates, and influenced social patterns more than the governments of the largest cities and states.

These transitions, though imperceptible to most of the people who lived in them, had dramatic, far-reaching effects. Some were highly desirable: The standard of living increased; the quantity, quality, and variety of goods available increased; leisure time increased. Other effects were not so desirable: Land was stripped; forests were laid waste; air was polluted; rivers were fouled; and a subtle new form of social indenture was devised—dedicated conformity to the employing organization.

Now we stand on the threshold of another transition—the emergence of the knowledge society. Production of the necessities of life—food, shelter, clothing, and other common material goods—will require the labor of a smaller and smaller percentage of the population. Now less than 3 percent of the population work on farms, and less than 12 percent produce all of our industrial output, while more than 30 percent go to school. These developments are the penumbra, the dimly lit half shadow of the future with which managers will have to contend. Although it may be difficult to predict the exact shape and form organizations will take, it is clear that managers will be concerned with what can best be described as a knowledge organization.

THE KNOWLEDGE ORGANIZATION

What is the character of a knowledge organization? On the surface several features are evident: (1) The ratio of knowledge workers to production workers increases rapidly. (2) The relationship between the two groups changes. Whereas in the past the knowledge workers were supported by the production workers, this reverses, and the production workers are increasingly dependent on the output of the knowledge workers. (3) Knowledge becomes the leading edge of the competitive effort. How knowledge is applied to products and markets determines the long-term expansion or contraction of the firm's production work force.

Less evident, but equally important, in the knowledge organization managers are aware that their firm is under unrelenting pressure to acquire and to use knowledge. They know that it is increasingly difficult, if not foolish, to base survival and growth primarily on ownership of scarce materials, on ownership of patents, or on temporary superiority in a market. They understand that product discoveries and marketing decisions made more than 5 years ago rapidly lose their ability to sustain the firm. Managers in a knowledge organization acutely sense that the major basis for economic growth and profitability lies in developing future managers who know how to guide an organization in the acquisition and use of knowledge.

The elusiveness of knowledge work

The essence of the knowledge organization is that work is done in the head. This means that knowledge work can't be seen. It does not fit into discrete, tangible units, and it is difficult to measure. Generally, managers with a traditional production, marketing, or accounting orientation find this difficult to comprehend.

Perhaps what most annoys and frustrates tradition-oriented managers is that knowledge work is nonlinear. It does not make sense to insist that a person should produce twice as many bright ideas in 2 hours as he produces in 1 hour. We cannot insist that the quality of a decision arrived at after seven people deliberate should be seven times as good as the decision made by one person. If we seem to be halfway toward the solution of a problem after 2 days, we cannot expect the complete solution in 2 more days. If the problem and solutions still seem unclear, does this mean that we will need another 2 days? Will we need more than 2 days? Or will the dilemma fall into place and will sensible solutions emerge in the next 2 hours?

The manager in a knowledge organization thus faces a life in which productivity is intangible and resolution is uncertain. It is hard for the manager to know when people are working. It is also extremely difficult for him to know when he has accomplished something. His knowledge has been fused with the contributions of so many others that it is often meaningless to identify his contribution.

Traditional methods of supervision emphasize regularity, measurement of work in process, and orderly appearance. When this form of supervision is rigidly enforced in the knowledge organization it may be not only ineffective but actually obstructive.

When we view the knowledge organization as a system, we can see four processes that should concern managers:

1. Finding and disseminating knowledge that already exists in the organization

2. Acquiring and creating new knowledge
3. Converting knowledge to profitable products and services
4. Managing people who work with knowledge

The first two will be discussed here; the second two will be examined in the next chapter.

FINDING AND DISSEMINATING
EXISTING KNOWLEDGE

The first job of a manager is to assemble and use the knowledge that already exists in his organization. A major difficulty is that existing knowledge simply does not move to the people who should get it. For years observers and consultants to organizations have been struck by how much people know and have thought about the problems and needs of their organizations. But they have been equally impressed with the difficulties of getting this knowledge to flow from where it is to where it can be used.

There are innumerable examples of the failures and near catastrophes that have followed from management's inability to use existing information. One case that received wide publicity is that of a well-known aircraft manufacturer that decided to build planes for the highly competitive commercial jet transport market. Top management felt that the opportunities for profit more than offset the high risk of the venture. As engineering design and model testing proceeded, it became clear to several members of middle management that the original cost estimates for the venture had been underestimated by a factor of no less than 4, and possibly as high as 10. Moreover, the company's lack of design experience with jet aircraft caused innumerable difficulties and departures from the original time schedule for completion of the first test aircraft. This information, which already existed within the organization, was diverted before it could reach top management. By the time it was allowed to reach top management, it was evident that a major failure was in the making. The information was no longer news: It simply confirmed what no longer could be hidden. The company suffered a severe economic setback; losses were so great that the company was on the brink of insolvency. There was widespread contraction in employment, and confidence in top management was shaken.

In another company, a research organization, several managers estimated that it costs more than $2 million and takes about 2 years to stop a project that is failing. It takes that long for people in the organization to "leak" negative information to top management.

In still another situation, a long-range plan had been developed to guide the future of a major food-growing and marketing company. Top management refused to follow the plan, apparently because it would involve fundamental changes in the company's competitive strategy and in its top organization structure. The company suffered economic decline for several years until, in desperation, the board of directors brought in several new top managers. The long-range plans that existed were dusted off and put into operation. The company's competitive strategy was redirected from growing and transporting products to developing new food products and to creative marketing. Over a period of 4 years the company became a highly effective, profitable organization.

Organizations today can be viewed as caldrons of knowledge—rich with ideas about new products, new processes, new approaches to markets, and new ways to improve management's effectiveness.

In such organizations, withholding, diverting, or ridiculing existing knowledge becomes the greatest source of current error. Isolating, ostracizing, or punishing those who present adverse information and analysis becomes the major source of future error.

Some hard-nosed questions

Recognition of the organization's dependence on knowledge is an essential managerial attitude. In addition, however, managers should be asking a number of hard-nosed questions about existing knowledge:

1. What knowledge is worthwhile?
2. Who in the organization has or should have it?
3. Who should receive this knowledge? Why? What are they expected to do with it?
4. How can we improve the way we collect and disseminate existing knowledge?

The question "What knowledge is worthwhile?" deserves further discussion. It is particularly troublesome for most managers. Some find themselves uninformed on the one hand and overinformed with useless data on the other hand. The manager in the knowledge organization must understand the various qualities that make knowledge valuable.

Worthwhile knowledge reduces uncertainty when a decision is made. Knowledge that does not reduce uncertainty is either redundant or irrelevant.

Worthwhile knowledge may also have a different quality: It may clarify where uncertainty cannot be reduced. It is extremely important for the manager to know what things cannot be known. Also, the manager should know what knowledge is so costly that for decision purposes it must be treated as an unknown.

However, rather than seek knowledge in general, as if by amassing a great enough quantity a decision will emerge, the manager must be able to pinpoint the kind of knowledge that is needed. Two simple questions can guide the manager to vital information:

1. How much would current conditions have to change for me to change my decision?

2. What information or conditions, not presently known, would cause me to change my decision?

Worthwhile knowledge may also have the quality of suggesting additional areas for search. In other words, worthwhile knowledge will describe the limits of its usefulness. It will clearly point out that beyond these limits we do not know whether all, part, or none of our current knowledge is usable.

The value of relevant questions

Interestingly, knowledge does not come only in the form of answers and objective data. In management, there are few things as dangerous as a comprehensive, accurate answer to the wrong question. This is pseudoknowledge. It easily misleads management into erroneous actions. Pseudoknowledge has mushroomed with the advent of computers, which have made available masses of data that answer questions managers found too costly to ask before. In too many instances, however, the data are collected but not used because they answer irrelevant questions.

It is vital to understand that in the knowledge organization, worthwhile knowledge may take its highest form in the framing of relevant questions. Formulating the right questions becomes increasingly a crucial function of the manager.

Distractions from this function may carry a high, hidden cost. For example, consider the psychological value of redundant knowledge. Many managers gain an increased sense of confidence and comfort from data that continually confirms what they already know. They frequently want "all the data" so that they can "get a feel for" trends and identify irregularities. Actually, their decisions rarely change as a result of these additional data. In the knowledge organization, supplying managers with redundant data can become a costly burden. In one organization, an executive estimated that he and his colleagues spend no less than

80 percent of their time preparing and polishing reports that tell upper managers what they already know. They have little energy or opportunity to formulate or study new, relevant questions.

ACQUIRING AND CREATING NEW KNOWLEDGE

It is evident that knowledge is rapidly becoming the firm's primary instrument of progress and competition. Existing knowledge defines our productivity and competitive skill in the present; new knowledge determines our productivity and competitive skill in the future.

Acquiring and generating new knowledge, however, is one of the great uncharted areas of management and human behavior. Indeed, if there is one place we need new knowledge, it is in how to get new knowledge. Managers, for example, need to study how they themselves generate new knowledge. In addition, they should be supporting research on the process of how we obtain and discover new knowledge.

Knowledge is new in two different senses, and it is important to distinguish these:

1. Knowledge may be new to one firm but known to others.

2. Knowledge may be new to one firm and *not* known to others.

This distinction between "new only to me" and "new to all others including me" suggests different approaches to getting new knowledge. The first indicates a strategy of acquisition. Search of literature, meetings with others, and negotiation are ways to obtain knowledge that already exists for others but is new only to me. The second indicates a strategy of creation. Speculative thinking, imaginative leap, and original insight are needed to invent knowledge that is new to all including me. From a managerial point of view these are two very different processes.

Often they can be performed only by completely different people.

All new knowledge has "stress potential." Conventional ways of thinking, well-established relationships among people, and the power to make decisions may be severely disturbed by new knowledge. Two extreme—but particularly dramatic—examples of how new knowledge can be upsetting are Columbus' concept that the earth was round when everyone believed it was flat and Copernicus' concept that the earth revolved around the sun when everyone believed that the sun revolved around the earth. Acceptance of the idea of a round earth stimulated an era of exploration. It made possible a national strategy of colonialism, it upset economic relations among nations and shifted competition to naval efficiency. Copernicus' concept raised so many questions about theologies founded on the idea that the earth is the center of the universe that the well-established relation between people and the church and the distribution of power between governments and the church could never again be the same.

Managers favor new knowledge. Like most of us, however, they want its promise but not its dislocations. Hence, the strategy of acquiring new knowledge from others is fraught with mixed motivations. On the surface this strategy is deceptively straightforward. It simply says search out and get from others the new knowledge they have. Of course, competing corporations deliberately want to conceal new knowledge from each other. But in the same corporation divisions are often more dedicated to concealing new knowledge from each other than from competing corporations.

Strong forces aroused

Managers should understand that efforts to acquire new knowledge arouse strong attracting and repelling forces. At the outset it is not clear which set of forces will prevail. When we lack knowledge and attempt to acquire it from others, four types of resisting forces may be triggered:

1. We did not invent the new knowledge; therefore, it is suspect—not relevant, not applicable.

2. Disdain for the organization, or division, that originated the new knowledge may prevent us from seeing the merits of the new knowledge. To do so would require us to change our unfavorable image of the originator.

3. We may fear that accepting the new knowledge will be seen by higher management as evidence of our inadequacy.

4. We fear disruptions may follow use of the new knowledge—possibly decreased need for our capabilities, adverse changes in the organization structure, reduction of our influence.

Thus the simple intention to acquire new knowledge can stimulate a deep core of resistance.

On the other hand, awareness of existing knowledge that we do not have can arouse strong attracting forces. Probably the greatest motivator is management's concern that if we lag our competitors too much, too long, we may not survive. Second, some people in the organization will see in the use of the new knowledge benefits for themselves—greater responsibility, increased influence. Finally, the originator may have an established reputation as a capable, forward-thinking organization or person. Then doubts are resolved in favor of the new knowledge. The reasoning usually is that, "There must be something in it we do not understand, otherwise someone as smart as Mr. X (or organization X) wouldn't be doing it."

THE MANAGER'S ROLE

Clearly, the manager plays a crucial role in efforts to acquire new knowledge. It is his job to encourage his people to search, to sense, to scan, and to expose themselves to as many sources of new knowledge as possible. Failure to reach out regularly for existing new knowledge leaves an organization vulnerable. It greatly increases the probability that management will be unaware of significant trends in new knowledge, will be making inappropriate decisions, and will not know how to look for new knowledge even when it wants to. Consider the case of American Woolen Company, once king of the woolen fabric business. The company earned peak profits by meeting delayed demand for woolen fabric during the 5 years after World War II. Then after steadfastly ignoring knowledge about weaving synthetic fibers and blends for 30 years, it declined into bankruptcy. By the time management wanted to reach for new knowledge, it didn't know how.

When it comes to creating new knowledge, the manager confronts a strange and different world. Gone is the stability, order, and reliability so essential to the daily recurring activities of the corporation. Instead there is the unusual, wondrous world of discovery and unpredictability.

The creation of new knowledge depends on several supporting conditions. Managers will find their concepts and skills severely tested when they attempt to provide these necessary conditions. Outstanding among them are:

1. Support for creative deviance
2. Immersion in existing knowledge
3. Unstructured time
4. New perspectives
5. Unusual groupings

Creative deviance

First, to create new knowledge means to depart—often radically—from conventional knowledge. Many half-formed concepts and irrelevant ideas have to be cast up before we can sift out an occasional nugget of worthwhile new knowledge. In any effort to create new knowledge the manager's first task is to develop a climate that supports creative forays. These ventures in imaginative thought must be departures from the known, the accepted. New concepts will deviate from the commonplace—indeed, they must if they are to be meaningful additions to the known.

The creative process is different from its final output—the creative product. The process flourishes in a climate that encourages deviant ideas—a climate in which it is understood that many ideas will be generated but few will pass the test of rigorous critical analysis. The manager must expect false starts. He must be prepared for vigorous argument today for concepts that are discarded as worthless tomorrow.

Immersion in existing knowledge

Creating new knowledge depends on being familiar with what exists—that is, if one wishes to avoid laborious rediscovery of what is already known. Robert Oppenheimer, the noted atomic physicist, would often say that adding to our knowledge in physics was not as difficult as most people thought. He said that first one must learn the language of the subject—the mathematics, the concepts, and the experiments, all of which were available knowledge. This might take a great deal of time and dedication, but after it had been done the process of adding to knowledge in physics, he said, was about the same as it would be in another field. Although Oppenheimer, with characteristic modesty, understated his talents, his point still stands: Immersion in and absorption of existing knowledge is an important precondition for the creation of new knowledge.

Unstructured time

People need unstructured time to pursue creative activity. They need adequate freedom from routine, repetitive activities that lull the senses, use energy, and occupy the mind with trivia. This is not to say that a regular schedule of work time is inappropriate. Quite the contrary. Productive discoverers of new knowledge follow a regular work schedule regardless of whether or not they feel creative. However, they tend to work excessively long hours when they think they are on the brink of a breakthrough; they often need time to recuperate and to rearrange their thinking after these intense episodes that frequently turn out to have been false starts. Unstructured time doesn't mean time without work. It simply means time in which structure—that is, goals and methods—emerges as we explore and work.

The creation of new knowledge depends on guarding unstructured time. It must be kept free of routine, programmed activities. Managers in knowledge organizations often create great difficulties for themselves here. If they continually succumb to pressures for near-term, measurable output and do not preserve some unstructured time for themselves and their work team, they undoubtedly are efficiently managing the obsolescence of their activity.

New perspectives

By systematically taking different positions, roles, or locations, when viewing a problem, one often discovers new knowledge. For example, it is well known that the same situation when viewed by managers of different functions, such as marketing, manufacturing, finance, and personnel, will elicit different definitions of the problem and different solutions. The idea is to capitalize on these differences. Because managers do not encourage taking unusual points of view, the organization frequently loses access to new knowledge.

Managers made great advances in new knowledge when they began to encourage thinking of situations from the viewpoint of people outside the organization. One great leap occurred when they asked, "How would I see this product if I were a consumer?" This was followed by "How would I see this product if I had to service it? If I had to install it? In this mass consumption society, with its growing population, managers are beginning to realize that they ought to ask "How would I see this product if I had to dispose of it?"

Taking unusual points of view can be systematically encouraged. Synectics, a method intended to encourage creativity, does just this.[1] For example, it asks people to explore military and political analogies to the problem being considered. Sometimes it asks them to think as if they were something in nature with characteristics similar to those in the problem—an animal, a tree, a geyser. The method may ask people to imagine that they are the real object. Consider this illustration from a team working on new products for a surgical manufacturer. "If you were an open wound what would you see? How would you feel? What would you want?"

Behavioral research long ago established that difficult problems are more likely to be solved by people who alter their points of view. It is now a matter of implementing this in the management of knowledge organizations.

Unusual groupings

Exchanging ideas with people who think differently than we do stimulates the discovery of new knowledge. The manager in a knowledge organization must take the lead in establishing unconventional groupings. People with different ways of conceptualizing a problem stimulate new approaches to knowledge in each other. Research discloses that the most productive scientists gain new perspectives by regularly discussing their ideas and problems with experts in fields different than their own.

The manager in the knowledge organization must learn how to encourage and guide unusual groups. Such groups pose a difficult opportunity: How to capture the creativity in diverse views without falling victim to the conflict? The search for new knowledge by groups composed of different managers and specialists is demanding. We refer to these intellectually high-powered groups as "brain trusts" and "think tanks." But, regardless of the irreverant names, they are an unusually rich source of new knowledge.

2. From Knowledge to Action

T he business organization is a social instrument. It exists to perform an economic function for society—to provide desired goods and services, and earn a profit. Ultimately, however, a corporation must use knowledge. It must apply knowledge to make new, or better, or less costly products and to make more effective use of its capital, material, and human resources.

The process of converting knowledge to action is the engine that drives the organization. But it is difficult for a manager to determine what knowledge is worth converting. He is pulled in different directions by his organization, by competing organizations, and by his vision of the future. Consider the following case from a major consumer goods industry.

Shortly after World War II, top management of a firm that was a leading producer of soap flake products for home laundering was asked to approve a project for the development of a home laundry detergent. Much was known about the physical and chemical properties of detergents, but up to that time they had been used almost exclusively in industrial processes. A major use was in separating and concentrating ore particles by "flotation"—a process in which pulverized ore is mixed with detergent-laden water. The ore particles adhere to bubbles formed by the detergent, float to the top, and concentrate in the froth that flows over the side of the tank. At the time there was no home laundry detergent.

Because of the company's long, successful history with laundry soap flakes, top management decided against the development project—a clear decision not to convert existing knowledge. About the same time another soap manufacturer, with a smaller share of the market, decided in favor of conversion. Approximately 2 years later it introduced the first detergent for use in home laundering. The detergent manufacturer swept the market, displaced soap flakes and kept a major share of the market for at least a decade.

OBSTACLES TO CONVERSION

Lack of knowledge frequently is not the major obstacle to conversion. Often, for various reasons, available knowledge is not converted to action. Sometimes the reasons relate to strategy. For example, a firm with a large market share may believe that introducing a new product will excessively cannibalize sales of existing products. Or a firm may be unwilling to introduce a new product because it has not fully recovered its investment in plant and equipment.

Sometimes the reasons relate to the organization's leadership. If the majority of managers at headquarters come from one division, they may not understand or value proposals from unfamiliar divisions.

Sometimes conversion is blocked for social and cultural reasons. For example, knowledge about how to improve productivity in underdeveloped countries is available, but there is strong resistance to applying this knowledge when it upsets established power relationships between fathers and sons, men and women, or government and religious leaders. Apparently these social and cultural obstacles to conversion were underlying factors in the deposing of the Shah of Iran in 1979.

Sometimes converting knowledge depends on beliefs about how work should fit into the scheme of life. Union attitudes toward work can severely limit the conversion process. This is a continuing problem even in a developed country like England where labor unions play a key role in the conversion process.

ANALYZING THE CONVERSION DECISION

The conversion of knowledge is a separate, distinct process. It is a transition, a crossover from the realm of thoughts and information to the realm of actions and things. It requires systematic analysis. The fact that an organization seeks a profit provides only one limited guideline. The following difficult questions and rejoinders illustrate the complexity of the conversion decision.

What are the customer's needs? This assumes "the customer" can be identified and his relevant needs can be described.

How will converting this knowledge contribute to the organization's goals? This assumes that organizational goals are well defined and that we can accurately predict the outcomes of the conversion decision.

What is the economic efficiency of this conversion proposal? This assumes ability to forecast economic results, behavior of competitors, and general economic conditions.

How does the conversion proposal fit into the organization's plans? This assumes existence of comprehensive plans.

What are the human and social costs and benefits of the conversion proposal? This assumes that we can identify and measure social costs and benefits. It assumes that managers wish to consider the indirect, moral consequences of conversion decisions.

Different answers

Even though organizations may compete in a common environment, they often answer the conversion questions differently. Consider the different approaches to international banking followed by American banks during the 1960s.

Although America's deficit balance of payments restricted the outflow of credit, international banking was the fastest-growing department in many banks. Some American banks became key sources of information about business, politics, and finance in foreign countries. They used knowledge to attract and hold customers among corporations with overseas business. Other banks converted their knowledge into ingenious financial arrangements that allowed loans to be made to foreign governments and firms without violating credit restrictions. Still others acquired knowledge of sophisticated operations research methods and used it to efficiently manage their portfolio of foreign assets.

CONVERSION STIMULATES
BOUNDARY CONFLICTS

Organizations often separate knowledge people from operating people, so the people who "know" are in one group and the people who "do" are in another group. Staff people are loosely coupled to "line" people; functional experts are ambiguously linked to operating managers. The boundary between the two groups is constantly under pressure as each attempts to influence the other.

Knowledge conversion increases intergroup stress. It precipitates conflict and may lead operating people to isolate themselves from staff. Frequently there is a battle over who has final authority, when the real issues are: What are the right questions? What are the best answers?

One approach to managing boundary conflict in knowledge conversion is to appoint coordinators or liaison agents. The persons appointed to this intermediary role, however, must be extremely skilled in the behavioral aspects of knowledge conversion, otherwise they introduce another obstacle. If they are not competent, they are ignored or at best humored by both camps. If they have formal power and are not skilled, they can so complicate and obstruct knowledge conversion as to bring it to a complete stop.

In one organization, for example, a "coordinator" was appointed with formal authority over a research group and a development group. At first each group attempted to form a coalition with the coordinator against the other group. In the interests of harmony, the coordinator gave each group the impression that he was on its side. Unwittingly his behavior confirmed the idea that there were "sides" and each group increased its intransigence, believing that it was simply a matter of getting the coordinator to "straighten out" the other group. This continued for several months.

In an effort to extricate himself, the coordinator practically eliminated all meetings between the groups and ordered that all communication go directly to him. He would decide how differences would be resolved. Both groups were frustrated and angry. They communicated only the information he asked for, which frequently was not adequate or relevant for the knowledge conversion decisions that had to be made. Instead of aiding knowledge conversion, the appointment of a coordinator introduced an impediment.

Managers and specialists have to be trained in the intricacies of knowledge conversion. Some organizations systematically use exchange assignments. For example, in one company selected managers in the research division exchange positions with selected managers in the production and marketing divisions. In some cases product development managers exchange positions with production managers and marketing research managers exchange with sales managers. Rotation, while not a complete solution, is an important step toward managing the boundary conflicts of knowledge conversion.

Closing the gap between the application of knowledge and the acquisition of knowledge is a challenge to every organization. One answer is to include people oriented to knowledge conversion in the early stages of a project. The presence on a team of one member who thinks early about resource allocation, commercial feasibility, and effects on the organization greatly helps the knowledge conversion process.

FACILITATING ACCESS
TO KNOWLEDGE

The organization must aid, rather than hinder, a manager's ability to review the knowledge guiding current actions. For example, when product designs or marketing plans originated by higher managers are not appropriate to the current environment, the discrepancy usually must be referred up the chain of command. Consider this illustration: In a manufacturing company, when production had difficulty assembling parts which according to engineering design should fit together, the problem was passed up the authority ladder in manufacturing. Managers primarily observed the chain of command and secondarily dealt with the problem. Their behavior often complicated simple problems, led to overreactions, and polarized factions. Knowledge conversion suffered, and manufacturing costs increased. There was high spoilage, high scrap, excess work in process, and lower-quality output. Manufacturing had resigned itself to these conditions as unchangeable. The organization ponderously attended to production problems and slowly ground out solutions.

The matrix organization and the multiconnected network offer better ways of gaining access to the knowledge needed to deal with this type of problem. They operate as follows: When a manager has a problem implementing an important action based on knowledge obtained from other managers, he may convene a meeting without passing the issue up the chain of command. In the production example, the production foreman could call a meeting of representatives of engineering, quality control, and purchasing. Matrix and network organizations recognize that converting knowledge to action sometimes depends on immediate access to relevant people regardless of where they are in the chain of command.

At higher levels of management, knowledge and understanding often diverge substantially from actions, and there is even greater need for access and integration. The matrix organization accepts the formal hierarchy but encourages crossing functional boundaries and levels of authority.

In a knowledge society, managers must work directly with each other to resolve knowledge conversion problems. *Knowledge-based organizations require managers to be problem centered rather than territory centered.* They need to reward problem solving and results rather than preservation of territory.

DEMAND FOR APPLIED KNOWLEDGE CHANNELS DISCOVERY

We have assumed so far that management has the knowledge it needs and the problem has been to convert it to useful activity. But what if management does not have the knowledge it needs? Then, management's demand for knowledge to convert affects greatly the discovery of new knowledge.

There are two hypotheses about what leads to the discovery of new knowledge. (1) The serendipity hypothesis: New knowledge results from accidental events. For example, Charles Goodyear discovered vulcanization by accidentally dropping rubber into a fire. (2) The demand hypothesis: New knowledge results from search programs in response to specific demands for knowledge. We learned how to design spacecraft that could return to earth without disintegrating and how to land and support men on the moon because that's what we decided to do.

The serendipity hypothesis may have been acceptable when science was less advanced and there were few large organizations. But, in a complex knowledge society the demand hypothesis more accurately describes reality. *This means that the manager's*

demand for knowledge principally determines the discovery of new knowledge. Thus the manager confronts an awesome question: *What new knowledge do we want?*
There is much we do not know, but given our limited resources, what do we want to know? Because we primarily find the knowledge we demand and little more, the manager's decision regarding what knowledge to search for is critical.

MANAGING PEOPLE IN A KNOWLEDGE ORGANIZATION

Although people are vital to a knowledge organization, they are also more vulnerable. They are subjected to new, intensive stresses which require new responses.

Power does not assure access to knowledge

In a production organization, the manager has the power to direct subordinates and often is expected to do so even in detailed aspects of work. By firmly using his managerial power he avoids being considered weak or incompetent. He can reward compliance by giving salary increases, attractive assignments, and promotions.

Strangely, in the knowledge organization, a manager who forcefully asserts his power to direct is often seen as weak. The manager's quandary is that directing others does not give him access to their knowledge, especially if they are demotivated by his assertion of control. Yet the manager must protect his legitimate power and cannot avoid his responsibility for ultimate outcomes.

The manager has less freedom to use straightforward directive power when processing knowledge even though he still has the power to reward others. The source of a manager's power shifts to the correctness of his knowledge and his ability to understand and use the knowledge of others. Thus, although the manager has formal hierarchical power, he must keep it in reserve for resolving conflicts. So long as there are no unresolved deadlocks, knowledge should guide action. This is not simple, and in practice there is constant tension between authority based on position and authority based on knowledge.

Stress and coping

Knowledge-processing organizations differ from traditional production organizations by requiring continuous, rapid formation and abrupt dissolution of work teams and task forces for special projects. These temporary social systems sporadically come into and go out of existence. They illuminate some needed knowledge or knowledge conversion and then fade. But the formal hierarchy endures. Most managers and specialists divide their time and energy across several projects. They are central in some projects and peripheral in others, but vital to each.

In the production organization, stress occurs as physical fatigue from boredom, monotony, and exertion. The production organization uses workers' muscles and ignores their minds. So the production worker seeks relief in spectator entertainment and mild mental stimulation.

In knowledge processing the diminished effectiveness of formal, directive power and the continuous participation in many overlapping temporary systems changes the stress people feel. In the knowledge organization stress occurs as mental and emotional fatigue from excessive variety in tasks, constantly changing relationships, and demand for unrelenting alertness and concentration. The organization uses the manager's and the specialist's minds and ignores their muscles. So they seek relief by participating in sports, physical activities, and mental diversions.

Physicians and psychologists are increasingly concerned about the manager's ability to absorb the stresses of the knowledge organization. There are many demands. Each alone is stressful, but together they may be overwhelming. The following five stresses stand out.

Situational Complexity. Goals must be defined and selected, but many are possible. No one goal alone is sufficient and priorities of goals continually change with events and accomplishments. Alternative courses of action must be created. Rarely can we devise an alternative without some undesirable consequences. Results frequently are affected by the actions of many other people whose goals differ from ours.

Ambiguity. It is increasingly difficult to attribute the results to our actions. Some outcomes are because of what we have done, but others may be in spite of what we have done. Cause and effect are often a matter of speculation, forcing managers to make the next decision either uninformed or, worse, misinformed.

Multiple Supervision. In addition to his formal superior, a manager must often contend with several other indirect but equally influential superiors who have the authority of knowledge.

Membership in Many Groups. A manager may have to start, build, and end effective working relationships continually in a changing series of project teams and task forces.

Vulnerable Self-Esteem. Knowledge is the fundamental commodity of the knowledge organization. It becomes increasingly difficult to separate evaluation of an idea from evaluation of the person who proposed it. Since even the best managers will propose some poor ideas, a person's self-esteem may be attacked at any time.

These five sources of stress typify work in a knowledge organization. They can't be eliminated, they can only be managed. But the human problems of knowledge processing have the potential to be extremely disruptive, painful, and costly.

SKILLS NEEDED

The manager will need knowledge and behavioral skills that are suited for knowledge processing. There are four that are particularly important:

1. Avoiding knowledge obsolescence
2. New concepts of structure and interaction
3. Consultative leadership skills
4. Understanding the attitudes and concerns of knowledge workers

Avoiding knowledge obsolescence

Although a manager has formal power to make decisions, he is limited by his ability to understand the implications of the knowledge communicated to him by subordinates, peers, and superiors. The rapid development of knowledge makes managers obsolescent if they do not continually update their knowledge. A production worker who lags in knowledge limits only his own opportunities, but a manager who lags in knowledge takes a greater toll. His power multiplies the consequences of his deficiency. He can obstruct the development of major segments of the organization.

Consider the following case. The Vice President of Finance of a manufacturer of specialized electronic equipment had not kept up with new developments in financial theory and practice. His department employed several bright young people with graduate degrees in business administration and with working experience in the use of computers in financial analysis. The knowledge these people attempted to use for the company's benefit made little sense to the vice president. He resisted changes in financial reporting and data processing that were by then commonplace in many competing organizations. Turnover was high among the knowledge competents. The vice president's decisions ignored sophisticated financial analysis and led to poor inventory decisions, inappropriate pricing, and misdirected market development expenditures. The company was purchased by a larger organization. Management of the finance area was gradually assumed by the parent organization as the lagging competence of the financial vice president became clear. Subsequently he was replaced and the department was reorganized.

Knowledge processing is particularly vulnerable to managers who wield formal power but who are *knowledge incompetents*. This is not to say that every manager should be more knowledgeable than his subordinates and peers. As knowledge advances, the manager must expect to lag behind others. Indeed, if he does not, the chances are that he is settling for mediocrity in his subordinates and is probably inhibiting their knowledge growth.

The manager's task is to continue his personal development to keep the gap in knowledge between himself and his team within workable bounds. He must be able to understand the consequences and the implications of the advice and information he receives. In a knowledge organization, few things are more destructive than the manager who uses his power to cut himself off from others to avoid exposure to knowledge he may not understand.

A knowledge organization also confronts managers with a new phenomenon—the arrogance of knowledge. Knowledge specialists may ascribe a degree of certainty to their models of the world that baffles and offends managers. Often the complexity of the world cannot be reduced to mathematical abstractions that make sense to a manager. Managers who expect complete, one-to-one correspondence between the real world and each element in a model are disappointed and skeptical.

Furthermore, most managers are conversion-oriented. They tend to be impatient with knowledge expressed as theory. They listen to a theory if it prescribes an unequivocal answer or a practical method, otherwise theories are considered irrelevant, pretentious abstractions. Managers are wary of pursuing knowledge without an immediate application in mind. Expenditures on searches for knowledge are accepted as a tolerable distraction when the firm is profitable, but mocked as impractical luxury when the firm is less profitable.

The conceptual gap between managers and knowledge specialists strains their relationship. Managers often consider knowledge workers to be naïve, insensitive, and arrogant. Knowledge workers often consider managers to be intellectually unsophisticated, defensive, and self-protective. Each obstructs and frustrates the other, and what was intended to be an infusion of knowledge degenerates into a series of skirmishes. The manager must be alert to this process, which becomes increasingly destructive as his knowledge obsolescence grows.

The manager has a right to ask for explanations of assumptions and theories behind knowledge. But he also has an obligation to use his powers to encourage pilot testing of knowledge that he does not have the conceptual training to understand. Illustration: Management of a major bank decided to build into its organization a "management science" group. The group received continual encouragement to study and if possible improve the bank's asset management policies and decisions. Over a period of several years, the group developed decision models that significantly assisted management. It is doubtful that any of the managers whose decisions determined the continued existence of the group understood, except in the most general terms, how the decision models were designed, tested and used. Yet, they continually sought the analytical outputs of the group and enthusiastically proposed additional decision situations for study.

Although the manager's knowledge competence limits his performance and affects his relations with others, he must expect many situations in which he will have to use his formal power. One important type of knowledge is knowing when we have insufficient knowledge. The manager must continually lead and press his team to identify what is not known. *One of the greatest dangers a manager faces in a knowledge society is not knowing the assumptions and the ignorance in the knowledge he receives when he has to make a critical decision.* When knowledge is not known or is unreliable, the manager must still make a decision, but at least he is aware that he must resort to intuition, judgment, and creative insight.

New concepts of structure and interaction

The manager's job will be to find ways to go beyond the knowledge limitations of the single human being. Businesses have become large and complex. Many employ thousands of people in intricate, mazelike organization structures. How such organizations acquire and use knowledge laden with different meanings often is not clear.

Knowledge, the major determinant of an organization's effectiveness, is not portrayed on organization charts or captured in organization manuals. The critical issue is: How can an organization avoid restricted, distorted flow of knowledge at crucial decision points?

For example, the knowledge the president of a large organization needs is increasingly beyond the capability of one human being. Traditionally, the president is served by layers of subordinates and buttressed with supporting staff and committees. Several organizations have experimented with a different structure to extend the capability of the president. They have devised a President's Office. It consists of a president and several equally competent top managers, each complementing the other's knowledge. Of course, this may complicate relationships and is not without problems. But it is an attempt to enlarge knowledge capacity by expanding our notions of structure and interaction.

Managers can expect organization structures to loosen, at all levels, encouraging increased interaction to aid the flow of knowledge. Every two or three levels of an organization may be viewed as a pool of knowledge and human resources. Each pool can be used to clarify goals and criteria relevant to its responsibilities and expertise. Temporary systems—groups with limited purpose and transient membership—may be formed from different pools to supplement the formal structure. We will discuss these concepts further in later chapters on "Collateral Organization," "Policy and the General Manager," and "The Board of Directors."

Consultative leadership skills

There will be heavy demands on the manager's leadership competence. He will have to adapt to many different people while working on unfamiliar tasks. *Inferior solutions to technical problems will be generated not so much because of lack of knowledge but because managers and knowledge workers may not have adequate consultative skills.*

For example: A headquarters staff marketing specialist had been invited by a regional marketing manager to review plans and methods in his region. The specialist unwittingly offended the regional manager on his first visit by publicly criticizing the region's performance and implying that the manager was at fault.

It was not politic to reject the specialist, so the regional manager and his staff spent the better part of a year compiling evidence to prove to headquarters that he was technically incompetent. Actually he was very competent.

Having failed to get adoption of any of his recommendations, he was on the verge of being recalled from the assignment. A behavioral specialist who had been working with the regional manager suggested a meeting with the marketing specialist to consider how they might work together better. At the meeting the marketing specialist described his disappointment over his inability to influence the organization. The regional manager then reviewed the evolution of their relationship and work and gradually came around to the felt insult of the first day. The marketing specialist was astounded. He had been completely unaware of the defensiveness his remarks had aroused. He thought that a little criticism would show people he knew the field and that he would not "soft pedal" adverse findings. With this incident out in the open the region was finally able to apply some of the marketing specialist's recommendations.

To improve his skills in working with others, the manager will want to consider the knowledge and educational programs available in group behavior. Relationships in a knowledge organization are more consultative than directive, so managers will need skills in giving and receiving help. A manager will need increased awareness of his feelings and how he expresses them. He will need to understand his style of dealing with conflict and how it affects other people. He will need listening skills to learn how he may better encourage search, creativity, and commitment.

Attitudes and concerns of knowledge workers

Recruits coming into knowledge organizations bring attitudes and concerns which change the culture of the organization. On one hand new recruits may seem cocky and belligerent. They have been trained in freedom of inquiry. Brought up on the discovery method—if you don't know, find out for yourself, develop and test your own theory, use your own reasoning skills, find your own way out of dilemmas—they challenge teachers, question the pronouncements of authorities, and are quick to find disparities between what people say and what they do. For many no question is unaskable, no authority or theory is beyond examination.

On the other hand, they may seem anxious. They often feel deeply concerned about socially responsible use of knowledge. They have read about or witnessed public dissent: labor strikes that violate laws, civil rights demonstrations, pro- and anti-war protests, impeachment proceedings against a president, environmental action protests. They have had to decide whether or not they personally would participate in some form of protest.

They have also had early opportunities to exercise responsibility. Many new recruits have been involved in student government programs that encourage self-direction in affairs that traditionally have been left to parents, to public officials or to school authorities. As a result, many have learned to dissent constructively and with responsibility. For example, at one well-known school of law, students decided that a course was needed in military justice and civil liberties. The faculty was not enthusiastic so the students arranged the course themselves, obtaining the services of several of the best authorities in the field. Although the course was noncredit, it was continued and additional noncredit courses were designed by the students.

Knowledge workers are continually concerned about opportunities for personal growth and for variety. They seek new challenges and have a need for accomplishment. Unfortunately many organizations ignore these concerns or are unable to fulfill them. The recruit may be told about opportunities, but often he gets unchallenging, repetitive assignments. Such experiences demotivate a knowledge worker.

Knowledge workers also continually need new education. They probably should attend a course or program every year. They also need assignments that stretch their capabilities. They may complain about overwork, but deep down they would not want it any other way.

Managers should understand that the morality of how knowledge is used greatly concerns knowledge workers. They feel deceived and embarrassed when their organization contributes to social inequities or international exploitation. They have theories of political economy, of government, and of social welfare. They do not stop thinking about these when they come to work. They recognize that neither government nor private organizations are infallible. Both need guidance in correcting injustices and controlling destructive practices. They especially want to minimize the adverse effects and inequities of their organization's activities.

In sum, knowledge workers are different from their predecessors. They are better informed, more skeptical, and more questioning. They are more accustomed to dissent and protest, more personally involved, and more inclined to action. The manager's task is to liberate and guide their drives for self-direction, for creativity, and for action.

3. Trust and the Decision Process

manager's first task in a knowledge society is to work with others to find and solve problems. But a manager's attitudes greatly affect how well he and others in his organization work together. A manager compresses his attitudes and impressions into one powerful belief—how much he can trust the other person; the other person, in turn, assesses how trustworthy the manager is. A manager's access to existing or newly created knowledge in his organization largely depends upon how much others trust him.

Ultimately, how much managers trust or mistrust each other significantly shapes their decisions. When they trust one another, decision quality improves and implementation is enhanced. When they mistrust, quality and implementation suffer.

Managers sense that they mistrust some people more than others, but they underestimate the corrosive effects of that mistrust. Ordinarily, they avoid discussing mistrust; instead they act on it. Avoiding the issue does not diminish the effects of mistrust; rather it disguises them, makes them less controllable, and more difficult to trace. To improve their decision process, managers must understand the meaning and pervasive effects of trust.

MEANING AND EFFECTS OF TRUST

Managerial disregard for the effects of trust seems to come from a misconception of what trust means. When questioned, many managers say that trust means friendliness—a feeling of affection, an expression of good will. In jest they may say, "It's a warm, cuddly feeling."

Trust, however, should not be confused with affection. The terms are quite different and failure to appreciate the difference causes much difficulty.

How trust differs from affection

Trust is the conscious regulation of your vulnerability to another person. The competent manager varies his vulnerability. He adjusts it for differences in the task, the situation, and the other person. Affection may, or may not, grow with trust. This is not to say that consideration for others and sensitivity to their needs is unimportant; it is only to say that trust differs from affection.

You may have affection for another person but still not trust them. For example, a parent may love a 10-year-old child but not trust him to drive the family automobile.

Furthermore, you may trust another and have no affection for them. For example, a passenger in a commercial plane may trust the pilot but have no affection for him. In short, trust and liking are not the same. Nor do they necessarily occur together. So, let us take a closer look at trust.

What is trust?

Trust consists of:[1]

- Increasing your vulnerability
- To another person whose behavior is not under your control
- In a situation in which the penalty, loss or deprivation you would suffer
- If the other person abuses or fails to protect your vulnerability
- Is substantially greater than
- The benefit, reward or satisfaction you would gain
- If the other person fulfills or protects your vulnerability

Consider this example. Parents show trust when they hire a baby-sitter so they can see a movie. Leaving their children significantly increases their vulnerability, and they cannot control the baby-sitter's behavior after leaving home. If the baby-sitter abuses their vulnerability, the penalty may be a tragedy that may adversely affect the rest of their lives. If the baby-sitter does not abuse their vulnerability, they will have the pleasure of seeing a movie.

How a manager shows trust

In business or government organizations, a manager shows trust when he discloses information he need not disclose. He increases his vulnerability when he reveals his goals, alternatives he is considering, his intentions, his problems, or his evaluation of personnel. Other managers may use this information to impede or undermine his plans.

A manager also shows trust when he seeks counsel from peers, superiors, or subordinates. He increases his vulnerability when he permits them to influence his decisions. He may be seen as a weak leader or some counselors may inadvertently or deliberately mislead him.

A manager additionally shows trust when he delegates. He increases his vulnerability when he depends on others to analyze a problem, gather information, or implement a decision. They may commit serious errors, delay implementation, or undermine his program. His reputation may be severely damaged, and demotion, transfer, or resignation may result.

Effects of trust

Trust determines the outcomes of many relationships, in addition to those among managers. Studies of relations between parents and children, counselors and clients, therapists and patients, and within problem-solving groups show that trust is critical to effectiveness.[2] Trust stimulates intellectual development and originality, and leads to greater emotional stability and self-control.

Among managers, trust facilitates acceptance and openness of expression. Mistrust provokes rejection and defensiveness. When working in a problem-solving group high in mistrust, managers have difficulty concentrating on tasks, and misperceive the motives and values of others. They distort what they hear and have less ability to recognize and accept good ideas.[3]

ELEMENTS OF TRUST

A manager expresses his feelings of trust (or mistrust) through *information, influence* and *control*.[4] We will examine each of these elements and describe how they act on one another.

Information

A manager who does not trust others will conceal or distort relevant information. He will withhold facts, disguise his ideas, and conceal his conclusions. He will hide feelings that increase his exposure to others. As a result, he provides incomplete, untimely information that inaccurately portrays reality.

Influence

The manager who feels low trust will resist other manager's attempts to influence decisions. He will suspect their goals, reject their views, and deflect their suggestions. He will deny or ignore their evaluation of results. Although he rejects the influence of those he does not trust, he will want them to accept and follow his views.

Control

Finally, a manager who does not trust will minimize his dependence on others because he feels that he cannot rely on them to abide by agreements. He will try to impose controls on their behavior when coordination is necessary to attain common goals. But he will resist their attempts to control his behavior and he will be alarmed by inferences that they may evade his controls.

When other managers encounter this low-trust behavior, they will hesitate to reveal information. They will reject influence and evade control. Their defensive responses will provide short-cycle feedback which reflects and increases his low trust. If neither party changes its behavior, the cycle will continue to repeat until the relationship stabilizes at a lower level of trust.

This downward spiral follows predictably from an initial lack of trust. There will be deficient exchange of information. Balanced, mutual influence will be blocked. Self-control will be displaced by external controls. Ultimately, problem-solving efforts will be less effective.

In contrast, when managers trust each other, the process is beneficial (see Fig. 3-1). Managers who trust reveal relevant, comprehensive, information. They make accurate, timely statements and contribute realistic data for problem solving. They

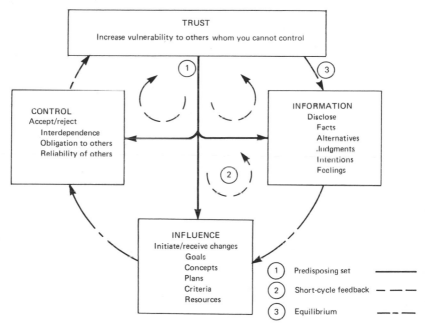

Figure 3-1. Trust and decision behavior.

have less concern that their exposure will be abused. They are receptive to influence from others and accept interdependence because they believe that others will abide by their agreements. So they have little need to impose controls on others.

Of course, managers must still have task competence or access to experts to solve a complex, technical problem. We shall assume that managers and their staff have adequate knowledge, experience, and creativity to solve complex problems. Their level of trust, however, determines their ability to locate needed competence and use it to solve problems effectively.

MISTRUST INCREASES UNCERTAINTY

A manager faces objective uncertainty in any problem. For example, important facts about the future behavior of competitors are unavailable or several key causes of demand cannot be identified. Low trust, however, adds social uncertainty to objective uncertainty. When managers withhold relevant information, distort intentions, or conceal alternatives, they introduce social uncertainty and increase the total uncertainty in solving a problem. Social uncertainty increases the probability that underlying problems go undetected or are deliberately avoided.

For example, in a paper company, low trust between marketing and manufacturing led to continued alteration and expansion of capacity to make a specialty product for a year and a half after marketing had overwhelming evidence that demand for the product was vanishing.

Managers have difficulty identifying and rejecting poor solutions. The socially caused uncertainty often leads them to grasp expedient, low-quality solutions rather than continue with unproductive, frustrating, problem-solving efforts.

On the other hand, trust minimizes social uncertainty. Managers feel free to disclose information when it is timely and to reveal alternatives when they are relevant. With little social uncertainty added to the objective uncertainty, managers can more accurately assess opportunities, risks, and the intentions of others. As a result, they can more easily identify underlying problems and are better able to design effective, creative solutions.

THE TRUST CYCLE

There is a trust cycle which shapes the relation of two managers with similar beliefs. (See Fig. 3-2.) If the manager lacks trust, he will disclose little relevant or accurate information, will be unwilling to share influence, and will attempt to control the other person. Assume the other also lacks trust. He will perceive the manager's initial behavior as actually untrusting and conclude he was right to expect the manager would be untrustworthy. The other person will feel justified in behaving with low trust. The manager, then seeing the other's responses as untrusting, will feel

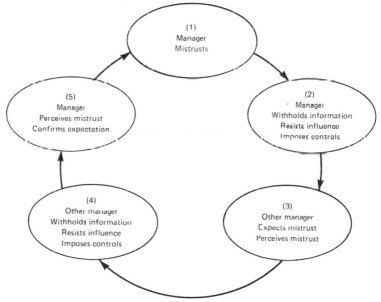

Figure 3-2. The trust cycle.

confirmed in his initial expectation that the other would not be trustworthy and will feel justified in behaving with less trust than when he entered.

They will continue around the loop, behaving with less and less trust, until they arrive at an equilibrium level of lower trust. Each will attempt to minimize his vulnerability and maximize his control of the other. The effectiveness of problem solving will suffer.

After several cycles, each will hold more firmly to his entering beliefs. Without a reliable basis for sharing influence, their mutual resistance will arouse frustration in both. If they have a deadline, one will attempt to impose controls while the other will try to evade them. If the manager is the other's superior, he will usually order compliance, which further reinforces the other's mistrust. By the middle of such a meeting the level of trust will be noticeably lower than at the beginning.

Fortunately, the trust cycle operates constructively when two people enter their relationship trusting each other. If one person minimally conceals, rejects, and blames, his behavior will support the trusting intentions of the other.

When people are unsure of how much they can trust each other, but they have important common interests, they can avoid escalating mistrust if one party listens and responds nondefensively. Then, the other's defensiveness is not aroused. Both are better able to understand the intentions and meaning of their messages. They become more problem-oriented and less concerned with controlling each other.

A STUDY OF TRUST

The case of Conrad Electronics (disguised name), a medium-size company with headquarters and manufacturing facilities in the northeastern United States, illustrates the effects of trust. The company designed and manufactured receivers, transmitters, amplifiers, and other specialized electronic equipment. It sold its products in several markets including the military, the government, original equipment manufacturers, and distributors who supplied retailers. The company had been profitable during World War II and into the middle 1950s with 55 percent of its annual sales on a cost-plus basis to the military and various prime contractors. Then military and government purchases declined, technology began to change, and the company faced increasingly strong competition.

In an effort to reverse its financial losses, top management cut the work force 25 percent. To bolster cash flow, capital expenditures were cut 75 percent. One year after these drastic steps, the company broke even. Then the board of directors replaced the president and the vice presidents of manufacturing and industrial relations. The former controller was promoted to president. Other insiders were moved up to the vice presidential posts.

During the next 2 years, the new management operated the company at a small profit. It earned 4 percent on net worth. But manufacturing facilities were increasingly obsolete each year. Although marketing was making progress in developing sales in the nonmilitary market, manufacturing was having difficulty meeting delivery promises. Work in process was high because the plant's old, multistory buildings imposed a poor plant layout. There was high turnover in the labor force. During the 3 years following the 25 percent reduction in the labor force, many superior engineering and production people left to take jobs with nearby competitors.[5]

Management's dilemma

The new top managers felt they were beginning to get control of the situation. They agreed that modernization and expansion of facilities was essential to the company's long-term success. But unknown to the vice presidents, the board of directors held a special meeting with the president in which it demanded improved profits next year. If this was not attained the board would ask for the president's resignation.

Under the circumstances the president tentatively concluded that modernization and expansion were not feasible in the short term. It would take more than 1 year to locate a new site, construct buildings, move equipment and people, and arrange the necessary financing. Also the board probably would not approve a heavy capital program. If anything, these activities would interfere with productivity and decrease short-term profits. The president had to meet with his vice presidents to announce his decision and formulate appropriate plans.

This case background was given to executives in the management development seminars of several major companies. Then the groups of executives took the roles of the president and the vice presidents of the Conrad Electronics Company and conducted the president's meeting. Other executives in the seminars were nonparticipant observers.

The managerial problems facing the Conrad Company were critical and complex. Small improvements in the quality of management's decisions and small increases in the motivation of managers would have great impact on results. The central problems required developing a strategy that would increase short-term profits without undermining long-term growth. And this had to be done with management support for short-term actions despite the vice presidents' disappointment over delays in modernization and expansion.

All the executives simulating the managers of Conrad Company were given identical financial and operating data. More than 80 different groups of executives worked on this case.

Half of the groups, however, were briefed to expect that they tended to mistrust each other as a result of their past 2 years of working together. The other half were briefed to expect that they tended to trust each other. The decision outcomes of the different groups clearly and consistently supported the model of trust we have presented.

Results of low trust

Low-trust groups resisted examining the situation in any depth. Instead, they blamed the president or the board of directors for short-sightedness. Usually, after much frustration, the president would forcefully issue edicts backed by implied threats of dismissal. The vice presidents would reluctantly agree to examine limited alternatives such as reducing the product line to further emphasize high-profit items or substantially reducing the labor force again.

Such behavior is common in low-trust groups under stress. They were defensive. They blamed others. They were unable to see the situation in its entirety. They were unwilling to accept responsibility for their part in the dilemma. They focused on the withheld goal of modernization and expansion. They had great difficulty considering other aspects of the situation and inventing other options.

When two vice presidents found they agreed, they joined forces to attack the president or whoever disagreed. These attacks polarized relationships and drove people further apart. Although some workable ideas were proposed, they were not heard or were rejected for spurious reasons. Each manager concentrated on protecting his area and pursuing only his interests. There was little attention to their interdependence. After the meetings the majority of managers were frustrated and said they would seriously consider employment with another company.

Results of trust

In contrast, high-trust groups analyzed the situation responsibly and creatively. They also recognized their disappointment over not being able to modernize and expand immediately.

They generated alternatives not requiring much capital in the short run but which could substantially improve profitability and aid their long-run interests. These included leasing nearby vacant manufacturing space and sourcing more semifinished or finished products. They would select promising new products and move them more rapidly from research into production. They agreed to revise their short-range and long-range plans and planned to present and discuss a new overall view with the board.

Their behavior exemplified that of high-trust groups under stress. They could deal creatively with new constraints and at the same time assist each other. They explored a range of goals, near-term and long-term. They could listen to many alternatives, select promising ones and shape them into workable courses of action.

They were supportive. They could use their differences to develop plans that integrated the functional areas—marketing, manufacturing, finance, and so on.

They balanced short-term constraints with long-term needs and interests. After their meeting, the majority of managers said they would not consider employment with another company.

These results may sound unrealistic and overly optimistic. Actually the managers were realistic and hard-nosed. They were aware of the risks and the real possibility of failure. But they said the situation was not hopeless and they were willing to dedicate themselves to surmounting the difficulties.

Summarizing the effects of trust on problem solving in the Conrad case, we found that, compared with low-trust groups, high-trust groups: (1) exchanged relevant ideas and feelings more openly; (2) defined goals and problems more clearly and realistically; (3) searched for alternatives more extensively; (4) had greater influence on solutions; (5) were more satisfied with their problem-solving efforts; (6) had greater motivation to implement conclusions; (7) became more of a team; (8) had greater loyalty and less desire to leave for another job.

DETERMINANTS OF TRUST

There are several elements that lead a manager to trust or mistrust others. The first two concern the manager himself. One is the nature of his personality. The other is the formal training he received for his specialty.

Personality

In childhood all of us have to depend on parents, other family members, and sometimes strangers. For some managers that childhood dependence was not fulfilled reliably. For others it was not fulfilled at all, and in some unfortunate instances it was abused and exploited. Understandably such managers, as adults, attempt to limit their vulnerability to others. They try to control relationships to minimize their dependence. Some people have deliberately been trained into mistrust by their parents. They have been taught to withhold information, keep their own counsel, and never seek help. Some adults intentionally abuse a child's trust to drive home the lesson that "you can't trust people."

A manager's personality inclines him to be trusting or mistrusting. It is important that each manager know his inclination because under stress his personal tendency to trust or mistrust will increase.

Formal training

Each specialty emphasizes a different orientation toward trust. For example, law appears to stimulate skepticism and mistrust as a starting assumption. Lawyers must contend with the natural desire of a client to tell only what supports his position, to forget conveniently, and to omit or distort contrary information. Also, the adversary method encourages the lawyer to withhold information from his opponent, revealing only what he is forced to disclose. In short, he is oriented not to trust his client or his opposing attorney.

In contrast, specialties such as physical or biological science orient people to accept what others say. Scientific investigation is based on reporting results accurately. A scientist who distorts results is readily detected and loses esteem. Scientists are trained to reserve judgment until they can replicate what others report, and if subsequent studies do not confirm the claims, scientists attribute the difference to faulty original research rather than mistrust the integrity of the original investigators.

Each business specialty such as financial control, marketing, or manufacturing instills a different orientation to trust. It is useful for the manager to be aware of how his particular, specialized training has oriented him toward trust. For example, accounting or finance may especially incline a person to mistrust financial data because of familiarity with how reports may vary from actual conditions.

In addition to personality and training, both of which are enduring and difficult to change, several other important elements affect trust. In most managerial situations these other elements are the major determinants of trust. Fortunately, they are accessible to managers and can be changed. They consist of:

- The competence of others for the task at hand
- Openness with relevant information
- Ability to respond supportively and nonexploitively
- The reward system
- Beliefs about the other's intentions

Competence

A manager's willingness to trust another person depends on his estimate of the other's competence to perform a specific task. For example, a manager will avoid assigning a neophyte to planning a critical, expensive national marketing program.

The manager continually assesses the competence of his subordinates and advisers. He varies his level of trust with his estimates. When a manager has a low estimate of a subordinate's competence, harmony and friendliness will not reduce his mistrust.

The manager must deal with the problem of helping the subordinate improve his competence, if he is ever to trust him. Otherwise the manager must reassign or replace the subordinate. Until the subordinate's competence improves, the manager will limit his vulnerability and will restrict the subordinate's assignments and responsibilities.

Openness

Our willingness to trust another manager depends on how open he is with *relevant* information. Some managers have an amiable, casual style which they mistakenly believe will lead people to trust them. For example, they cultivate easy conversation and friendliness. They are open with their views of political or social issues of the day. They discuss their family concerns and stimulate enjoyable debates of current events. In business problem-solving meetings, however, they withhold or distort *relevant* information.

Their restriction of relevant information impedes and confuses others while maintaining advantage and control for themselves. There may be a time lag, but eventually other managers and subordinates invariably discover the individual who withholds or manipulates relevant information. Then, regardless of his openness with *irrelevant* information, they mistrust him.

Supportive response

Our willingness to trust another manager depends on his ability to respond supportively and nonexploitively to our vulnerability. We increase our vulnerability by revealing facts about our situation and by disclosing our analysis, opinions, and judgments. We increase our vulnerability further by revealing our concerns, intentions, and feelings about a situation.

We trust others who respond supportively—that is, who accept us and our right to have the concerns, opinions, and feelings we have.

Supportiveness does not mean that they must agree with our views. Rather, it means that they can express their disagreement without ridiculing, humiliating, or embarrassing us. They can disagree with our views but do so without diminishing us as persons. Supportive response means that others do not use our exposure to deceive and subsequently take advantage of us.

In a trusting decision process, managers can openly disagree without reducing each other's self-worth. Also, they do not feign agreement to conceal their views and later exploit what they have learned.

Reward system

Our willingness to trust others depends on the reward system. If competition is rewarded, then trusting the other person is clearly not in our self-interest. In such a win-lose reward system, our gain is the other's loss and the other's gain is our loss. For example, two divisions of the same company may compete to sell similar products to the same customer. Each division is rewarded for maximizing its sales and profits. There is little incentive for each to trust the other. Managers will resist sharing product and market information across divisions because they see their relation as win-lose.

In contrast, a joint reward system encourages trust. In a joint reward system our gain is also a gain for the other person. Our loss is also a loss for the other. For example, if a division makes a major sale, all departments share the benefit. If it loses a major customer, all departments suffer some loss. In the joint reward system the shared payoff or loss makes it advantageous for managers to trust each other. Trust helps them maximize their mutual gain and minimize their mutual loss.

Most managers are in a mixed reward system. They determine which way the balance of trust will tip. For example, sales, manufacturing, and research departments compete for limited funds. They compete for manpower and capital but at the same time jointly benefit from sales. In one company, department managers competed for resources so strongly that they had great difficulty collaborating for their common benefit. Employees described the organization as a collection of fiefdoms under jealous barons.

In long-term relationships, when departments are interdependent and the reward system is mixed, managers who mistrust will maintain only enough openness for uninterrupted operation of their department. In such an organization, combined efforts that might exploit beneficial opportunities are rare. They are too difficult to orchestrate.

Intentions

Finally, our trust depends on our beliefs about the other's intentions. Our belief determines how we interpret his behavior. If we believe the other manager intends to exploit our resources or diminish our power we will be suspicious. We will be skeptical even if the other manager is open and supportive and we benefit from joint activity. We interpret his trust as a ploy to get us to lower our defenses.

If we believe the other person has malicious intentions, we interpret trusting behavior as clever deception. Thus, although the other manager may be trusting, our beliefs may lead us to see in his behavior evidence of harmful intentions.

On the other hand, if we believe the other manager's intentions are constructive, we overlook mistrust. We treat mistrust as a temporary lapse attributable to stress or oversight. We do not revise our beliefs about the other's good intentions until we suffer significant damage.

ZAND'S LAWS OF TRUST

The implications of this discussion can be summarized by several laws of trust.

1. Low-trust groups can self-destruct

Managers in a low-trust group operate with incomplete information, distorted interpretations, and suspicion of each others' intentions. As a result they make decisions with an inaccurate picture of reality. They have inadequate awareness of risks. Their mutual suspicion limits them to a restricted set of alternatives designed to minimize their vulnerability. Such alternatives usually do not respond creatively to the situation. Managers who work in a low-trust group will try to resign from the group. If they cannot, they find a pretext to circumvent the group's decisions or reasons to dissolve the group.

2. Low trust drives out high trust

Managers who are trusting increase their vulnerability. They disclose relevant information and express their true judgments and intentions. Low-trust managers take advantage of this exposure to the detriment of the high-trust managers. To defend against repeated exploitation, the high-trust manager is driven to low-trust behavior. He withholds information and disguises judgments to decrease his vulnerability.

3. Rapid growth masks low trust

When an organization is growing rapidly and sales and profits are increasing faster than average, managers are caught up in the demands of sustaining growth. They need expedient solutions to current problems. There are many promotion opportunities and managers stay in one job only for a short time.

A manager concentrates on showing that he is ready for promotion by solving current problems with quick fixes. With short tenure in a position, the manager expects to move to a new job before having to confront the effects of low trust in the current job. When the organization's rate of growth decreases, however, the movement of managers to new jobs slows. Then the effects of low trust linger and cannot be handed off to an unsuspecting successor.

4. Increasing the level of trust is a slow, complex process

Reward System. It makes little sense to demand trust when the reward system is clearly and totally win-lose. Such a complete opposition of interests can only foster low trust. In a purely competitive market, low trust between organizations may be acceptable when it stimulates efficiency and innovation. Within an organization, however, the benefits of competitiveness and low trust among components of the organization must be carefully weighed against the costs.

If the manager wishes to increase trust, the system would have to be changed toward mixed or joint rewards. This is a necessary step. Without it other steps will fail. Assuming the reward system has joint or mixed outcomes, then the manager can consider other ways to increase trust.

Increase Vulnerability. In this approach, the manager increases his exposure moderately, thereby signaling that he seeks a similar response from others. The increment should be moderate because other low-trust managers misunderstanding the behavior may initially exploit the new vulnerability rather than offer a matching increase in their exposure.

The process of tendering small exposures may have to be repeated many times. A major shift from low trust to high trust rarely occurs after only one or two exposures. Increasing trust requires a long period of offers and tests of sincerity. After increasing his exposure, it is important that the manager obtain a similar response from the other before proceeding further.

Relationship Analysis. Another more direct but more difficult approach is to analyze the sources of trust or mistrust in the relationship between managers. The managers discuss two key questions: What are we doing that decreases our trust of each other? What can we do to increase our trust of each other? Such a discussion probes issues beneath immediate, tangible business problems. This may be difficult because some managers become defensive, believing that trust is a personal matter not to be revealed to others.

Before attempting such a review, managers should have a common understanding of the meaning and effects of trust such as I have presented in this chapter. Also, it is helpful initially to have a skilled, impartial third person moderate and guide the analysis and discussion. The paradox is that managers must have some trust to be able to talk about their mistrust.

4. Collateral Organization

et us assume that managers have a workable level of trust and therefore should reasonably be able to gain access to each other's relevant knowledge. Then the organization becomes the focus of concern. Does the organization help or hinder the flow and use of knowledge?

NEED FOR INFORMED ADAPTABILITY

Usually, repetitive tasks and a stable environment move a firm along the experience curve toward greater economy in production, and increased efficiency in marketing. However, these conditions also frequently lead to a mode of organization which works against the future knowledge-processing interests of the firm.

It is important that managers understand why success may breed an organization with decreased ability to process knowledge. And, if the organization hinders knowledge processing, what can the manager do to help himself?

Most firms must operate in an increasingly turbulent environment. They are buffeted by unstable international relations among the major countries of the world, significant changes in military posture, and governments alternately constraining and then subsidizing certain economic activities. Markets are increasingly unpredictable because of erratic swings in foreign exchange rates, rapid technological breakthroughs sending new economic shock waves before the old ones have been absorbed, and so on. Managers are becoming increasingly aware that informed adaptability is at a premium and to attain it they may need different modes of organization to find and solve different types of problems.

SUPPLEMENTING THE FORMAL ORGANIZATION

This chapter describes an emerging mode of organization—a *collateral organization*. A collateral organization is a parallel, coexisting organization which a manager can use to supplement the existing formal organization. A collateral organization has different norms—that is, standards of behavior, methods of making decisions, and procedures—than those in the formal organization. The different norms are deliberately designed to make the collateral organization more suitable for identifying and solving problems which seem intractable in the formal organization. No new people are required and the collateral organization is carefully linked to the "regular" organization.

In parallel, not in place of

Some organization specialists contend that free-form organizations and participative leadership should displace hierarchical organizations and directive leadership.[1] Ideally, they say, knowledge rather than level of authority should determine decisions. Furthermore, they predict that the increasing complexity of the organization's environment will cause one-person decision making to give way to some form of group consultation and decision making. These views have merit, but the idea of totally displacing existing formal systems seems extreme to managers who simply want to improve their organization's adaptability and effectiveness.

There is increasing evidence that different structures and leadership styles are needed for different tasks. The superiority of any one approach above all others cannot be defended.[2] The key issue is: How can we help managers design effective, knowledge-processing, problem-solving organizations and use them flexibly?

COLLATERAL MODE

Research into the relation between the structure of a problem and the effectiveness of different organizations suggests that a manager should use more than one mode of organization. To state it simply: Authority/production-centered organizations work best with "well-structured" problems; knowledge/problem-centered organizations work best with "ill-structured" problems. These organizational modes and problem structures will be described later. The point is that since problems vary in structure, managers can and should use more than one organizational mode. The word "organization" is used to mean the communication channels, relationships, and inner workings of a group composed of a superior and his subordinates, and the working relationships between such groups.

The secondary mode of working will be called a collateral organization. Hence, a collateral organization is a supplemental organization coexisting with the usual, formal organization.* Of course a manager may develop more than one collateral organization, but to keep matters simple we will talk of only one collateral mode.

Typically, a work group has a chain of command and a division of responsibilities designed primarily for coping with well-defined, repetitive problems. But continual changes in consumers' desires, competitors' tactics, and product technology introduce unforeseen, ill-defined problems and opportunities. The

---

* Collateral, when used as a noun, denotes assets pledged as security for a loan. It is used here as an adjective, meaning to exist at the same time and level as, hence in association with, another organization.

hierarchical organizational structure is not designed to discover and solve these "ill-structured" problems. Managers therefore need collateral modes regardless of organizational level.

Understanding and acceptance

Managers hesitate to depart from the formal hierarchy to use a collateral mode because they have difficulty explaining and legitimizing such departures. Traditional organization theory, for example, offers only the vague concept of "informal organization." Managers are advised to avoid or suppress the informal organization because it is unreliable and unpredictable.

The manager's confusion is sometimes compounded by development programs which focus on improving his skill in individual and group behavior, but rarely introduce relevant organization theory. For example, one manager tried his new leadership knowledge in his formal organization, by encouraging open questioning of goals and discussion of methods. He temporarily blurred the formal boundaries between jobs. Other managers interpreted his actions as undermining authority and disrupting the formal organization. They resisted and discarded his changes. The manager was in a theoretical limbo. Without concepts, he could not explain to others what he was doing in terms they could understand and accept.

The concept of collateral organization is an aid to managerial understanding and organizational efforts to make better use of knowledge.

MATCHING PROBLEMS AND MODES

A problem is a dilemma and an organization is an instrument. It is useful to think of a problem and an organization as a set which is poorly or well matched. If the manager is to choose the right instrument for the job, it is important to know when a problem and an organization are matched.

The structure of problems

A problem can be classified as either well structured or ill structured. Some problems of course will have characteristics found in both categories, but analysis of the pure types will contribute most to understanding the matching process.

A well-structured problem—for example, preparing a customer's bill from a list of items and prices or putting values into a computer program which calculates the present worth of a capital investment—has the characteristics of physical or routine mental work.

In contrast, an ill-structured problem—for example, determining what new products should be added to a line over the next 3 years, preparing a schedule of prices for products that do not exist in any market, or projecting the long-range organizational, financial, and employment effects of a new marketing strategy—has the characteristics of complex, nonroutinized mental work. The elements of well- and ill-structured problems are outlined in Table 4-1.

Usually a manager assumes that he has only one organization which he must use for all problems. That is like a carpenter who assumes he can use only a hammer for all jobs. An effective manager first classifies a problem and then chooses an organizational mode best suited for it.

Modes of organization

An organization (work group) can be classified as (1) authority/production-centered or (2) knowledge/problem-centered. Of course, some organizations will cross both categories, but again we learn the most from studying the two pure types. The authority/production mode is concerned with mobilizing people and equipment to maximize output of a finished product or service. The knowledge/problem mode is concerned with processing or inventing knowledge to solve problems. Elements of the two organizational modes are compared in Figure 4-1.

Table 4-1 Characteristics of well-structured and ill-structured problems

Element	Well-structured problems	Ill-structured problems
Variation of output with hours of work	Known Proportional	Unknown Nonproportional
Variation of output with number of people	Known Proportional	Unknown Nonproportional
Characteristics of input and output	Countable Quality accurately measurable Errors detected quickly, precisely	Not countable Quality difficult to measure Errors difficult to detect
Information available	Relevant Accurate Complete	Uncertain Inaccurate Incomplete
Solutions	Few are feasible All are known Best one determined easily	Many are feasible Few are known Best one difficult to determine
Experts	Past solution of similar problems is a reliable indication of expertise	Many claim to be expert, but past experience is an unreliable guide to expertise
Methods of control	External standards such as output targets, hours allowed, cost goals can effectively control performance	External standards are inapplicable and misleading
Feedback about results	Occurs shortly after action Can be attributed to the action	Occurs long after the action Cannot be attributed only to the action

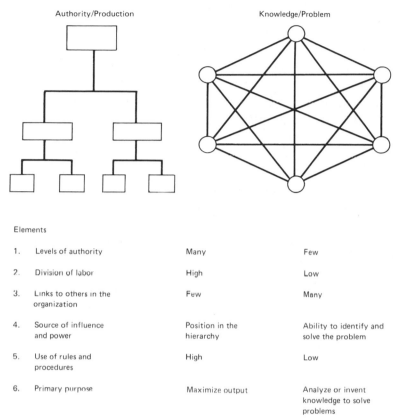

Authority/Production   Knowledge/Problem

Elements

1.	Levels of authority	Many	Few
2.	Division of labor	High	Low
3.	Links to others in the organization	Few	Many
4.	Source of influence and power	Position in the hierarchy	Ability to identify and solve the problem
5.	Use of rules and procedures	High	Low
6.	Primary purpose	Maximize output	Analyze or invent knowledge to solve problems

Figure 4-1. Types of organization.

Effectiveness of different combinations

Experimental research with small groups suggests that some combinations of organizations and problems are more effective than others. For well-structured problems, groups in the authority/production mode produce more output, more rapidly, than groups in the knowledge/problem mode.[3] Also, when groups in the knowledge/problem mode are given well-structured problems and are allowed to reorganize, they shift to the authority/production mode. They install a hierarchy, divide labor, and cut unused communication links.[4]

For ill-structured problems, however, groups in the knowledge/problem mode devise solutions of better quality, more rapidly, than groups in the authority/production mode.[5] The hierarchy, the division of labor, and the rules that make the authority/production mode effective for well-structured problems seem to interfere with the group's ability to devise quality solutions to ill-structured problems.

Another characteristic of the authority/production mode makes it less suitable for ill-structured problems: It tends to reject unsolicited innovation. Managers react to uninvited proposals for improvement as distractions that may reduce output. In contrast, the knowledge/problem mode tends to accept and use unsolicited innovations to improve productivity.[6]

There are no experimental data on whether authority/production groups shift to a knowledge/problem mode when they face an ill-structured problem. However, studies of actual authority/production organizations indicate that when confronted with an ill-structured problem, such as entering a volatile market undergoing rapid technical change, managers do not shift to another mode but tend to redefine the problem, forcing it to fit the existing hierarchy and division of labor. Companies unable to shift to the knowledge/problem mode were unsuccessful in the new environment.[7]

The most effective combinations (see Figure 4-2) are well-structured problems with authority/production organization (Quadrant I), and ill-structured problems with knowledge/problem organization (Quadrant III). The other combinations (II and IV) are not so well matched.

Shift to a secondary mode

There is little likelihood that the authority/production mode, which is characteristic of most business organizations, will vanish. It works for well-structured problems and sustains the organization's efficiency. There is, however, a limit to how far it can be stretched. When a significant problem keeps recurring, that limit has been exceeded. The challenge is: Can a manager and his

Type of problem	Type of organization	
	Authority/production	Knowledge/problem
Well-structured	I High output Rapid processing Small number of errors in output Members low in authority report low satisfaction Tends to reject unsolicited innovations	II Lower output Slower processing More errors in output More satisfying Accepts unsolicited innovations
Ill-structured	IV Lower output Slower processing Low-quality solutions Low in creativity Orderly, but not functional	III High output Rapid processing High-quality solutions High creativity Appears disorderly, but is functional

Figure 4-2.   The relationship between type of problem and type of organization.

group shift to a secondary mode before their primary mode becomes ineffective? If they cannot, *the organization itself becomes an impediment* adding further complications to the original problem.

Events in a large southwestern oil refinery illustrate the point. During the years when petroleum prices were less than $5 a barrel and supplies of gasoline and heating oil were plentiful, the refinery had developed a hierarchical organization and work groups geared to continuity of input. Although parts of the refinery were periodically shut down for scheduled maintenance, unexpected breakdowns occurred regularly. These unscheduled breakdowns significantly reduced the refinery's throughput. Managers of the departments and sections of the refinery repeatedly expressed three common beliefs: (1) the breakdowns could not be foreseen; (2) repair of the breakdowns invariably depended on several other departments; (3) after a breakdown all that could be done was being done and the repair time could not be shortened.

Several years later prices had increased manifold, industry refining capacity was lagging behind demand, and petroleum supplied to the refinery was varying. Each additional day of refinery downtime had increasing effect on company earnings and on supplies to consumers. Still, the managers adhered strictly to their hierarchical structure and their original perceptions of the problem. A new refinery manager familiar with how others had been dealing more effectively with breakdowns was disappointed. He estimated it would take almost 3 years of prodding and contention to make some inroads on the problem. He said, "I am as concerned about this organization as I am about the breakdowns. We will first have to modify how the managers think and work together before we can do something creative about the breakdowns."

RELATION OF COLLATERAL ORGANIZATION TO FORMAL ORGANIZATION

In the remainder of this chapter, we shall assume that the formal organization is in the authority/production mode. The collateral organization will be the knowledge/problem mode. This state of affairs may of course be reversed in some organizations such as research units and educational organizations.*

---

* When the knowledge/problem mode is primary, the organization requires and attracts individuals who value individual contribution, creativity, self-motivation, and low interdependence. Going from a knowledge/problem mode to an authority/production mode introduces complex problems of coordination, reduction of individual freedom, group operation, and conflicts with personal values. It is not simply the reverse of going from the authority/production mode to the knowledge/problem mode.

In tandem

A collateral organization is distinguishable from and linked to the formal organization as follows:

1. The purpose of the collateral organization is to identify and solve problems not solved by the formal (primary) organization.

2. A collateral organization creatively complements the formal organization. It allows new combinations of people, new channels of communication, and new ways of seeing old ideas.

3. A collateral organization operates in parallel or in tandem with the formal organization. Both the collateral and the formal organizations are available. A manager chooses one or the other, depending on the problem, A collateral organization does not displace the formal organization.

4. A collateral organization consists of the same people who work in the formal organization. There are no new people.

5. The outputs of the collateral organization are inputs to the formal organization. The ultimate value of a collateral organization depends on successfully linking it to the formal organization, so its outputs are used.

6. A collateral organization operates with norms (that is, expectations of how people will behave) that are different from the norms in the formal organization. The different norms facilitate new ideas and new approaches to obstacles.

Characteristics

A collateral organization has the following characteristics:

1. All channels are open and connected. Managers and specialists are free to communicate without being restricted to formal channels in the hierarchy.

2. There is rapid and complete exchange of relevant information.

3. Norms encourage careful questioning and analysis of goals, assumptions, methods, alternatives, and criteria for evaluation.

4. A manager can approach and enlist others in the organization to help solve a problem, without being restricted to his formal subordinates.

Applications

The two cases that follow illustrate different approaches to introducing a collateral organization.

SILVER CITY BANK

Ralph Brady, vice president of Silver City Bank,* was concerned about future strategy for the international banking department. It was 1968 and he wanted to improve the department's ability to compete with well-established competitors in a changing, worldwide market. At this stage in his thinking he felt the issues, problems, and opportunities were ill structured. He discussed his concern, in general terms, with his superiors, who encouraged him to recommend changes in strategy.

His work group functioned primarily in an authority/production mode. He and his subordinates were amiable and cooperative and deeply involved in getting work out. Although there was the glamour of international travel and negotiating loans of large dollar value, most of the situations were well structured.

Mr. Brady discussed strategy with several key subordinates but felt he and they were not able to dig into issues in any depth. Each could focus only on short-term obstacles close to his own group's productivity. The ill-structured problems of analyzing long-term strategy seemed to elude the problem-solving capability of his group. Finally, Mr. Brady consulted an organization

---

* Names in this case and the one that follows are fictitious.

specialist who had been working with another department in the bank.

The specialist interviewed Mr. Brady and his division managers. He observed that their daily work required many immediate decisions and was extremely demanding. They could not be away from a telephone. He concluded they would have great difficulty establishing the relationships needed to identify and solve the ill-structured issues of strategy. Although the managers were competent problem-solvers with extensive knowledge of international banking, they could not direct their skills toward analyzing strategy. Somehow, they would have to depart from the norms of their intensive authority/production-centered work.

Preparing for a collateral mode

The specialist explained the need for a collateral organization to Mr. Brady and his group. He proposed an initial 3-day meeting, at which strategy and operating issues would be discussed, analyzed, and if possible resolved. The men were so busy they insisted it be from Friday afternoon to Sunday evening.

Aware that collateral organizations frequently fail because managers may have unrealistic expectations and cannot foresee the difficulties of a collateral mode, the specialist stressed setting limited, attainable goals. He suggested that the group try to identify key issues but discuss only two or three priority issues in detail. Since there would be many unanswered questions after the meeting, they would also have to approve some structure which could be used to work on finding answers after they returned to work. Finally they should discuss how they could organize to solve ill-structured problems more effectively in the future.

Ten days before the meeting, the specialist interviewed each manager, gathering information for the meeting and answering questions about format. Each manager described the issues he most wanted discussed, the outcomes that would make him feel the meeting was worthwhile, and the difficulties that might interfere with managers' being reasonably open about important issues. The interview process itself stimulated managers to think about norms that departed from those of the primary mode, such as how they communicated, who they related to, and how they made decisions.

Learning the collateral mode

At the start of the meeting, the specialist made the following statements to clarify the norms of the collateral mode and to assure its proper connection to the primary mode.

- The power differences in the formal organization would still exist when the managers returned to work.

- Mr. Brady, the vice president, was the group's superior, and this was his meeting, not the consultant's.

- The group or its members could make recommendations, but Mr. Brady would have to approve any proposal before it could be implemented.

- Regardless of formal position, managers usually have valuable insights and proposals that cut across many different areas. It would be the responsibility of the higher managers to facilitate expression and use of these views.

- The specialist would suggest procedures and ask questions to help the group identify, analyze, and solve problems.

Opening the channels

The specialist then reported a summary of the issues managers wanted to discuss. At first, the group operated in an authority/ production mode. Managers frequently proposed solutions before a problem had been clearly defined. The specialist made process observations to alter these norms. Discussion was brought back to managers whose views had not been heard adequately. There was regular testing to ensure that any problem was understood by all before solutions were discussed in depth.

Regardless of status, managers began contributing important information and insights. This helped the senior managers see how the open channels of their collateral mode improved problem solving.

Evolution of collateral mode

On the second day, the managers decided to continue to experiment with their collateral mode after they returned to work. They would set aside "unstructured" time—multichannels, free questioning, and so on—to study several ill-structured problems. Based on their new experience, they also adopted a special norm for their collateral mode: Incomplete ideas, although not thoroughly reasoned and defendable, were welcomed. This was a deliberate and significant departure from behavior in their formed organization. It was intended to stimulate search and creativity. They reiterated, however, that in the hierarchical (primary) organization, a recommendation would still have to be supported by thorough reasoning and documentation. Thus, they had grasped the distinction between primary and collateral modes without falling into the trap of insisting that one had to displace the other.

Connecting to the formal organization

After returning to work at the bank, Mr. Brady and his group used their collateral mode to analyze ill-structured problems one morning each week for the first 6 weeks. This helped stabilize the collateral mode and increase cohesion. They worked out a long-term agenda, which they used to form several task forces for specific problems. The daytime meetings were conflicting with work, so they reviewed their needs and shifted to one evening a month. They also convened 3-day, off-site meetings at 5-month intervals to review progress and react to task force reports. The task forces made proposals to Mr. Brady and the full group during the year. Gradually a comprehensive international banking strategy was formulated.

There were differences of opinion within the task forces, and sometimes there were conflicting responses to reports from the task forces. The process had its difficulties, and in two instances Mr. Brady encouraged and arranged for the transfer of two individuals who were personally dissatisfied by and unable to contribute to the collateral mode. In general, the managers at this level were bright and aggressive and enjoyed the opportunity to do a better job of planning their department's future. At their daily work, the nature of their activities, however, impelled them toward an authority/production mode. Incidentally, this did not mean that they were not caring, friendly, and thoughtful of one another and their subordinates.

In any case, the primary and the collateral mode were quite distinct. Managers were well aware of the different properties of the two modes and when one or the other was in use. The department was relatively autonomous and top management stayed out of its internal activities, so the use of the collateral mode caused no problems and raised no outside concerns.

Results

The original stimulus for the collateral organization was the need to develop a strategy for international banking. No before-after measures were taken of attitudes, perceptions, share in influence, or other variables. At the time, gathering such data was not a primary concern. Nevertheless, in terms of the critical criterion—quality of the strategy—the decisions made in 1969 were impressive, considering subsequent political and economic developments in Latin America, the Far East, and Europe in the 1970s.

The group decided to expand in Latin America and the Orient, where competition was thin, demand was growing, and the bank could effectively use its existing relationships to tap an expected increase in U.S. trade with countries in those areas. In Europe, where competition was heavy for the existing large market, a strategy of affiliating with strong foreign banks and selectively establishing a few home office branches was instituted.

Organization and development plans

To support the new strategy, relations between international banking officers and domestic banking officers who served U.S. companies with large overseas affiliates or subsidiaries were reviewed and significantly improved. Procedures in the bank's main European office were also substantially changed, facilitating more accurate and rapid responses to customers. The department's formal structure was changed to fit the new strategies. Several divisions were eliminated, others were combined. Finally, a manpower development plan which systematically rotated upcoming managers to selected world areas and headquarters assignments was instituted. For at least a decade after 1968, top management rated the international banking department's performance outstanding each year. Mr. Brady was promoted to senior vice president and a subordinate moved into his job.

Of course, without control groups we cannot assert that an equally good strategy would not have developed without a collateral mode. Using Mr. Brady's group as its own control, however, we recall that it had repeatedly tried to formulate strategy while working in its primary mode but had been dissatisfied with the results.

Another interesting result is that the collateral organization concept spread during the 3 years following its initial use by Mr. Brady. Each of his five division managers developed collateral organizations with their own subordinates.

Summary

To recapitulate, the collateral mode in this case unfolded through several steps and had several components.

• The manager, Mr. Brady, used a consultant who diagnosed the situation and proposed consideration of a collateral mode when after several attempts, the primary, formal organization did not resolve the problem of formulating an acceptable, long-term strategy.

- The manager met for 3 days away from work with his subordinates, a peer from Europe, and the consultant. They tried and used new norms of communication, relationship, analysis, and decision making while identifying issues and developing tentative priorities.

- The manager and his subordinates continued to meet weekly using the new norms. They came to agreement on key strategic issues. They spun off task forces composed of themselves and some of their subordinates to study selected issues.

- The total group continued to meet monthly and quarterly.

- The task forces, in their work, used the new norms to supplement the conventional norms of the formal organization.

- The task force reports were presented and discussed in the full group.

- After further consultation with the group and then his superiors, the manager formulated a long-term strategy.

- The manager's subordinates—each of whom managed a unit of the division—had continually discussed implementation of different strategies while on the task forces and in the full group. After Mr. Brady announced the accepted strategy—which came as no surprise to anyone—the unit managers simply and naturally used the new norms when appropriate in their day-to-day relations in the formal organization as they implemented the long-term strategy.

- The norms of the collateral mode were maintained, and used as needed, by periodic meetings away from work. Several unit managers subsequently introduced a collateral mode in their units.

From the summary above we can see that a collateral mode is a more complex system than a task force. Frequently, however, a collateral mode may spawn task forces. The important point is that the collateral mode introduced new norms which were carried into its task forces. Also, the new norms ultimately enriched the primary, formal organization. In addition, in many formal organizations, a task force is composed of people who normally may not work together and who are temporarily released from their jobs to work full time on the task force. In contrast, in the Silver City Bank case, the collateral mode consisted entirely of people who normally worked together. And, none were released from their jobs to work on a task force.

AJAX CORPORATION

Now we turn to the introduction of a more complex, multistage collateral organization. Again the purpose is to illustrate the usefulness of a collateral organization and to outline some methods for introducing one.

Fred Anderson, manager of the Maintenance and Laboratory Service Division of Ajax Corporation, a large research and development company, was concerned about the cost effectiveness of his unit. His division had been performing more work with the same budget, and although objective standards were difficult to establish, he felt improvement was possible. Since the Service Division employed 300 of the 3000 people in Ajax, it was a major expense.

The Service Division had been formed 2 years earlier by consolidating into one unit activities that had previously been performed by small groups in each of the major research and engineering divisions of Ajax. After consolidation, the foreman's job changed from supervising only craftsmen in one specialty, such as machinists or electricians, to supervising a team which could completely build and repair complex laboratory facilities. Thus, at the level of the foremen and below, the organization took on some properties of a *matrix*. Specialized craftsmen were assigned to different projects as needed, and they usually worked on several projects with groups of varying size and membership. In addition, for the first time, foremen and craftsmen were rotated between the company's two locations, 20 miles apart.

Middle managers advised Mr. Anderson that the foremen were at the crux of the division's difficulties and would be the key to any improvement effort. They described the foremen as unwilling to stress high output, reluctant to discipline workers, resistant to cost reduction and work changes, and tending to promise work dates that frequently were not met.

Mr. Anderson consulted organization specialists, who observed that foremen were affected by the behavior and attitudes of their managers and that the problems Mr. Anderson was trying to solve were complex, ill defined, and substantially different from the well-structured routines of daily manager-foreman relations. The consultants proposed, and management accepted, a sequence of collateral phases involving both managers and foremen.*

Collateral phase 1

All 16 managers of the division including Mr. Anderson met for 3 days away from the plant to identify and solve work problems of concern to managers and foremen, and learn a collateral mode of problem solving.

First Day. In this collateral mode the managers worked on only one element of problem solving at a time, in a method called "staged problem solving."

First, the managers developed an inventory of problems while working in three "diagonal slice" groups—no manager and immediate subordinate in the same group. Next, in a plenary meeting of all the managers, each group presented its problem inventory. Then the groups developed a consolidated inventory. At first the managers were apprehensive about their peers or

---

* I wish to thank Matthew B. Miles and William O. Lytle, Jr., who, with the author, were the consulting team. We collaborated in writing an extensive, more technical report which is the basis for this condensed description.

superiors. They stated issues indirectly. Gradually, with the aid of observations by the specialists, small-group exercises, and the discipline of discussing each group's problems in plenary session, the apprehension disappeared.

Next each group diagnosed causes of a subset of problems. Copies of a written summary of each group's diagnosis were immediately distributed to all the managers. The managers met again in plenary session and each group explained and discussed its diagnosis. By the first evening the managers were deeply involved in the effort. Significant problems had been identified and causes were discussed without disguising names or incidents.

Second Day. On the second day the managers met in three peer groups. The groups were asked to: (1) assign priorities to problems; (2) nominate managers to task forces that would recommend solutions to Mr. Anderson at the meeting; and (3) nominate managers to a steering committee that would take control of the remainder of the meeting and also guide the collateral organization after returning to the plant and the hierarchical (primary) organization.

To assure that the collateral organization would tie into the formal one, the managers were asked to use the following criteria for nominating candidates to a task force: (1) at least one manager should have formal authority to act on the problem; (2) several should be technical and procedural experts on the problem; (3) at least one should know and represent the views of people who would be affected by a solution.

The managers elected a five-man steering committee and asked the division manager to serve as chairman. Thus, they connected the collateral organization's steering committee to the highest authority in their formal organization.

The steering committee formed task forces for the high-priority problems and assigned every manager, including themselves, to a task force. The task forces rediagnosed their assigned problems and developed solutions.

In plenary session, each task force presented and discussed its progress. All managers freely questioned, commented, and provided additional inputs. The task forces absorbed the new inputs and met again to refine their proposals. By the end of the second day involvement was intense. Groups worked late into the night to prepare their recommendations for the next day. These groups very closely followed the knowledge/problem-centered mode in Figure 4-1. Levels of authority had been telescoped, each manager was linked to all the others, influence was based on contribution and not on formal position, rules and procedures were minimized, managers several levels apart in the formal organization worked side by side intensively concentrating on the problems at hand.

Third Day. During the third day, each task force presented its recommendations in plenary session. To clarify that the organization was shifting back to its primary mode, it was explicitly stated that the Division Manager, Mr. Anderson, could respond in any of the following ways: (1) accept the task force recommendation, designate a manager to implement it, specify a completion date, and state how a report of progress would be given to all the managers; (2) suggest modifications, discuss them, and approve a modified recommendation; (3) withhold a decision, pending additional information or alternatives, and authorize the task force to continue its work back at the plant; (4) withhold a decision if in his judgment the proposal was not appropriate now but might be at a later date; (5) reject the recommendation and not give any reasons.

There was a good deal of excitement and joking as Mr. Anderson stood at the front of the room waiting to hear each group's statement of the problem, review of causes, and recommended solutions. During the presentations, managers freely called from the floor for clarification or elaborated a point when they felt it was misunderstood. The cohesiveness of the managers was noticeably higher than before the 3-day meeting.

By the third day much information that had been known only in isolated pockets of the formal hierarchy had been exchanged across the organization. Managers had demonstrated their trust through their open discussions during the preceding 2½ days. With this background, solutions that were not feasible or integrative were readily discarded in the task forces. As a result, the final recommendations were appropriate and well thought out. Mr. Anderson neither rejected nor withheld a decision on any of the recommendations.

Collateral phase 1 results

A new information system for managers was instituted. A new strategy for recruiting engineering and scientific specialists was approved. Middle managers were delegated additional decision powers. A task force was established to redesign the division's organizational structure.

The managers also made plans to follow up in the hierarchical organization problems they had identified but did not have time to solve during the 3-day meeting. Finally, they agreed they would join the foremen in a collateral organization if the foremen invited them. They also discussed how they might best work with the foremen in a collateral mode.

Collateral phase 2

One week after the managers' collateral organization experience, all 18 foremen met for 3 days at the off-site location. The managers' collateral organization was instituted first so they could decide from personal experience whether to approve a collateral organization for foremen. The managers had met without the foremen to prevent tension and distorted communication between levels from interfering with learning to work in a collateral mode.

The procedure and activities in the foremen's meeting were similar to the managers' meeting. Some minilectures and demonstration exercises were eliminated to save time, but in all other ways the foremen's collateral organization used the same "staged problem solving," small group discussions, and plenary sessions.

The foremen, like the managers, developed their own inventory of problems, diagnosed causes, set priorities, and elected their own steering committee to take control of their meeting. The steering committee established foremen task forces, which began work at the meeting. At first, like the managers, the foremen were apprehensive and indirect. Again with the aid of process observations, exercises, and the discipline of having to present their group's deliberations to all other foremen, the norms of the groups changed toward those of a knowledge/problem mode.

To link the managers' collateral organization to the foremen's collateral organization for work on common problems, the foremen invited the managers to join them the last day and a half. Contrary to management's stereotype of foremen as insensitive, the foremen invited all the managers to join them. All came except five who had to be left to run the division.

Joint Groups. A joint steering committee of managers and foremen assigned managers and foremen to joint task forces. Managers and foremen had agreed on many issues adversely affecting the performance of foremen. These included: confusion about foremen's authority to work crews overtime, to purchase inexpensive materials which were delaying completion of a job, or to grant workers time off; misunderstandings about the scope of the foreman's job; the need for a better system for screening and assigning priorities to incoming jobs; inadequacy of engineering services on complex, technical jobs; inadequacy of pay differentials between foremen and craftsmen; conflict about the merit pay system; the need for a better manpower assignment system; conflict about the training of foremen and craftsmen.

There was tension within the joint task forces as managers and foremen who knew each other by name but had never worked closely prepared to discuss problems that had been suppressed, distorted, or circumvented in the formal organization. Some foremen became guarded when a manager tried to dominate, but, the issues and the withheld information that had been constraining the organization were introduced via the"impersonal" written task force reports. During the third day, the joint task forces presented their recommendations to Mr. Anderson, in the same format as before. Mr. Anderson immediately made several important decisions. Procedures for working on unsolved problems after returning to the plant were also established.

Collateral phase 2 results

Foremen were given wider latitude to authorize overtime to complete a job without their supervisor's approval. They could also authorize workers' time off without pay. Foremen could purchase parts that were delaying job completion up to $200 per job without going through time-consuming, formal purchasing procedures. These measures helped cut costs and sped completion of jobs.

Mr. Anderson also decided that task forces concerned with the responsibilities of foremen, the training of foremen, the merit and performance review system, providing proper engineering support, and reviewing pay differentials between foremen and workers were to continue their investigation after they returned to the plant and the hierarchical organization.

Much misinformation about foremen attitudes and behavior had been dispelled, and managers had tested some of their stereotyped reactions to foremen and found them inappropriate. The outcome was a concerted effort on the part of both groups to provide the conditions that would enable foremen to be effective, rather than to blame them for inadequacies that were not under their control.

Thirty important problems had been identified, nine had been assigned to task forces, three had been resolved. Completion and review dates had been established for the others, and procedures had been developed for following through on the remaining problems. An attitude survey showed that managers and foremen felt they had learned much about one another and about problem solving. They were enthusiastic about the collateral organization.

Collateral phase 3

After returning to the plant and the hierarchical organization, task forces of managers, foremen, and joint membership continued their work. Progress was slower than expected because of daily work pressures.

There also was testing of the authority/production mode. Some foremen task forces, impressed with their new influence, attempted to circumvent middle managers and moved directly to the joint steering committee or the Division Manager with short-term work issues. Senior foremen quickly sensed the resentment this was arousing among middle managers and redirected the foremen task forces to the issues they had been assigned.

Managers of other divisions in the laboratory were skeptical about allowing foremen on task forces. They were concerned that foremen might usurp higher management's authority. Mr. Anderson was able to reassure the other divisions that this dual mode of operation need not spread to other divisions unless they wanted it. He was also able to convince them on the basis of preliminary results that the performance of the Maintenance Division would improve significantly.

Evaluation of collateral mode

Based on the ill-structured problems identified and solved, the collateral mode improved the organization's effectiveness. After nine months, six of the nine original high-priority and five secondary problems were solved. All but three task forces had completed their assignments and were dissolved. Work was to begin on 12 less-critical problems.

The collateral organization was self-operating; no organization specialists were used. One year after the first meetings, a new division manager, promoted from within the division, continued the collateral organization with the aid of the joint steering committee. Using small groups, a new inventory of problems was developed, three new task forces were formed, and progress was reviewed with the steering committee until the new problems were solved.

To obtain information about attitudes toward the collateral mode, interviews were conducted 18 months after the start of the project. Five managers and five foremen representing all levels of management, every task force, and both steering committees were interviewed. Each respondent felt strongly that the collateral mode was extremely useful and strongly supported its continuation.

COLLATERAL ORGANIZATION AND RELATED FORMS

These two cases, one relatively simple and the other more complex, illustrate uses of collateral organization. They can help us clarify the relationship between collateral organization and other forms such as "task forces," "temporary systems," and "matrix organizations."

Relation to task forces

In both Silver City and Ajax, each collateral organization included task forces. This can be misleading, because a manager may assume he can install a collateral organization simply by forming a task force. The important question is: Does the task force operate with norms different from those in the hierarchical (primary) organization? Many task forces, spun off by conventional hierarchies, operate in the same authority/production mode as the primary organization. Then, individuals pursue only their department's interests and minimally question goals, assumptions, methods, and criteria of evaluation. Such a task force often continues the restricted flow of information, condones the poor use of resources, and blocks creativity.

The task forces in both Silver City Bank and Ajax worked in a collateral mode. They had learned new norms in their off-site meeting. If they had not, it is doubtful that they would have contributed so creatively or enthusiastically.

In contrast, a task force operating with the authority/production norms of its formal organization often cannot fulfill its assignments and comes forth with low-quality unsatisfactory recommendations.

Frequently it has to be replaced by a second task force and sometimes a third one. The real problem is that the task force needs a collateral mode—a set of new norms—for itself.

Also, the task forces in Silver City Bank and Ajax were embedded in a larger collateral system that used knowledge/problem-solving norms. In contrast, conventional task forces are isolated attachments to a formal hierarchy using authority/production norms.

Relation to temporary system

A temporary system is formed with the understanding it will have limited duration. Its dissolution may be determined by (1) time (a two-day conference), (2) the occurrence of an event (the completion of a report), or (3) attaining a level of performance (a marketing unit solves its sales training problems without further aid from headquarters staff).[8]

A collateral organization terminates for one of two reasons. First, the ill-structured problems it is intended to solve are solved and there are no more. Second, the permanent, primary organization has absorbed the norms and the special competence of the collateral organization. In the second instance, the primary organization attains a new level of functioning, making the collateral mode redundant.

A collateral organization will be useful so long as it compensates for a deficiency in the primary system or it induces needed changes in the primary system. For example, in Silver City Bank the collateral mode was first used to fill a gap in the primary organization by intensively solving strategy problems for about a year and a half. Then it was used to induce change by guiding implementation for about a year. After that, it was activated at semiannual intervals to take stock of unresolved, ill-structured problems. It would be used more intensively if the problems were serious and not solvable by the primary organization.

Relation to matrix organization

A matrix organization is intended to provide a project or program manager with easier access to functional specialists. It often operates primarily in an authority/production mode, as in the Ajax case. A matrix increases internal competition for resources and intensifies conflicts over priorities and assignments among functional managers and project managers.[9]

These conditions stimulate managers to overstate needs, to hoard resources, to withhold information, and to block others from access to needed manpower—in short, to behave in an authority/production mode with high conflict. Thus, a matrix organization may itself need a collateral problem-solving mode. Some firms such as TRW Systems appear to have recognized the need for organizational development activities that build collateral modes to complement and assist their matrix (primary) organization.[10]

OPERATING PROBLEMS

A collateral organization tends to increase the use of groups, at least initially. It also puts more stress on middle managers and surfaces problems of individual tolerance and flexibility.

Need for groups

A manager may be concerned that introducing a collateral organization will increase the number of problems going to groups for solution. This may happen initially for two reasons. First, there appears to be a temporary increase in the number of problems, because a collateral organization identifies problems that were previously diffuse or unshared. Second, collateral organizations concentrate on high-priority, organizationwide problems, which are usually solved better by a group than by one person working alone. After an initial surge, the need for groups rapidly decreases, because the collateral mode diligently separates problems that should go to one manager (or a pair of managers) from those that should go to a larger group.

Stress on middle managers

When a collateral organization permits lower and higher managers to interact directly, the stress on middle managers increases. Higher managers may discover that middle managers have been distorting and editing the upward flow of information. Lower managers may discover they can influence higher management decisions more easily than they thought possible. Both higher and lower managers discover they need less time to identify and solve complex problems. Management may be prompted to redesign the hierarchical organization and redefine the role of middle managers.

In the Silver City Bank, after working in a collateral mode, managers discovered they could expand operations more rapidly than planned because an anticipated shortage of managers could be met by freeing several apparently redundant middle managers for other assignments. In the Ajax case, managers in the collateral mode concluded that several middle management positions were redundant but should be kept for backup purposes and for training.

Individual flexibility

Some subordinates have a strong need for structure and a relationship with their superior that does not change. They are comfortable only when working in one mode all the time—either authority/production or knowledge/problem solving. The important element for them is stability and consistency.[11] Even though problems may change and require organizational versatility, they find shifting from one mode to another confusing. Most subordinates, however, can be productive in more than one organizational mode, provided they understand the purposes of a collateral mode, know which mode they are in, and know when it will end.

Sometimes a superior may not have the flexibility to work in more than one mode. If this is the case, attempts to use a collateral organization will meet strong resistance. The majority of managers, however, seem to have enough flexibility to use a collateral organization. The achievements in the two cases described above were heavily dependent on the flexibility of Mr. Brady and Mr. Anderson.

Too often, a manager's skepticism toward attempts to introduce a supplementary organizational mode have been misconstrued as a sign of deep-seated, personal rigidity. This "rigidity" usually fades when the manager understands the concept of collateral organization. When he sees how it can productively complement the hierarchical organization without displacing or destroying it, he can be remarkably flexible. As a matter of fact, after a manager experiences his first successful collateral organization, the problem is usually not one of rigidity but of overoptimism. He feels he and his group have broken through to a new form of relationship and productivity, and he easily develops overly optimistic expectations of future accomplishment. The demands of daily work, however, quickly intrude, as they must, making continued use of the collateral mode an infrequent, disjointed activity. Some ill-structured problems are solved, but because of interruptions, solutions take longer to implement than he planned. New ill-structured problems that are identified take much greater effort to solve than the manager expected. He discovers that time for the collateral mode must be fought for and taken from the primary mode.

After using a collateral mode, the manager and his subordinates learn that the hierarchical organization can continue. Disorder does not take over. Directive behavior can still be used, but there is better understanding of how to integrate participation and group effort with the formal organization through use of a collateral mode. Perhaps most important, organization members learn concepts and methods which enable them to freely invent and use new modes for solving ill-structured problems.

PART 2

USING KNOWLEDGE

5. Marketing Management Behavior

t appears that the training and experience of marketing managers may prepare them to be good marketers but controversial, enigmatic members of top management. Although they tend to dismiss it, marketing managers, like other specialists such as financial managers and manufacturing managers, have knowledge-processing predispositions which concentrate their attention and inhibit their peripheral vision. When formulating policies or solving problems that cut across all functional departments, the marketer brings assumptions, concepts, and patterns of behavior that differ significantly from those of other managers. In top-management situations, where the goals and actions of different departments are highly interdependent and managers must work together closely, the marketing manager often appears especially provocative and perplexing. The question is: What is so different about marketing management behavior and why does it seem bewildering and amorphous to other managers?

CONSUMERS, MANAGERS, AND MARKETERS

Marketers are primarily interested in consumer behavior. They have to be to improve their marketing effectiveness. But, as they understand more about consumer behavior, marketers either ignore or implicitly assume that they also understand more about managerial behavior: specifically, the decision-making behavior of nonmarketing managers in large, complex, hierarchical organizations.

Understandably marketers explore consumers with unrelenting intensity. Consumers have been projected, probed, and prodded. They have been motivation-researched, attitude-researched, and action-researched. Their fantasies, their wishes, and their symbolizations have been examined. The latent meaning of their buying behavior has been laid bare. Marketers have even built psychological models of the buying process in which the buyer attempts to match his self-image with his image of a product or a brand. For example, a report on car-buying behavior describes the process as "an interaction between the personality of the buyer and the personality of the car."

At the other extreme, marketers have built mathematical models of consumer behavior using impersonal, quantitative data about consumer actions without theories of consumer motivation.

Clearly, marketing managers are concerned with the behavior of consumers. One might say they have a consuming passion for consumer behavior. The behavior of other managers, however, is often treated as an annoyance or an inconvenience. And, marketers seem particularly resistant to looking at their own behavior as managers.

Traditionally, the managerial behavior of marketers has been treated as a problem in organization structure. Questions are raised such as: How should the functions of marketing be divided? Where should they be placed? To whom should they report? What is the role of the product manager? The marketing staff specialist?

The main concern in this chapter is the beliefs, attitudes and behavior of marketers who move up to top management. What view of the world and methods of thinking do they bring? How do they seem to differ from other managers? What are the implications of these differences?

THE MARKETER'S POINT OF VIEW

The role demands of a marketer are quite different from those of a manager of any other function. In particular, there are six aspects of the marketer's role and his responses to this role that are critical.

External orientation

To the marketer the world of action and results is outside his firm. The people who are really important, the ones who in the final analysis determine whether his decisions are good or bad are not in the company. Who are these people? In the main, they are consumers, distributors, competitors, and government agencies.

Thus the marketer must think outward if he is to be effective. He must act as a link between his firm and many different subcultures. This is very difficult. He needs to know at all times the customs, beliefs, intentions and expectations of consumers, distributors, competitors, and government agencies. Under these circumstances, it is not unusual that the marketer has little desire to think of other managers in the firm.

In contrast to the marketer, managers of other functions can be almost entirely internally oriented. The significant people for them are mainly managers higher up in the chain of command and managers of other functions. Thus manufacturing, research, and finance can interact almost exclusively within and among themselves with occasional meetings with marketing managers. Of course, there are some contacts with outsiders such as scientists, bankers, and suppliers, but these are secondary to the prevailing internal orientation.

This is not to say that marketers are not also internally oriented—they are. But their internal orientation is secondary and instrumental. Relationships with other managers in the firm are valuable to the marketer only to the extent that they contribute to more effective marketing relationships with the important others *outside* the firm.

Mythical people

For all of his outward orientation, the marketer has great difficulty knowing who is really out there. Generally the marketer interacts with a myth, a figment of statistical imagination. Marketing research provides helpful clues, but in the final analysis the marketer's situation is much like that described in Socrates' allegory of the caves: a world in which one can see only the distorted shadows of others. This is especially true of the marketer's image of the consumer in mass markets.

Who is the consumer? For example, is it the Northeastern suburban housewife, with 2.8 children and a family income of $25,000? One can ask endless questions about the mythical consumer. Getting a meaningful, reliable picture is very difficult. How is this consumer like other consumers? Different from others? Why does she buy or not buy our product? Who will be tomorrow's consumer?

The marketer's life is complicated because there are no simple answers. Each question has many answers and each different answer is correct. There is a multiplicity of consumers. To reduce them to a usable abstraction is a continuing exercise in myth building.

Ambiguity in the marketer's world only starts with the consumer. Take competition, for example. We use the term as if there exists a single, well-defined firm or product that is *the* competition. Other firms in the market are competitors but not competition. The marketer's competition is a subtle composite—a psychological image compounded of the effects of competitors' advertising, promotion, product qualities, prices, outlet accessibility, distributor behavior, and many other factors. These images of competition are in the consumer's mind. To make the situation more of a fantasy we need only remember that we are not too sure who is the consumer. So the marketer must contend with ambiguity compounded with ambiguity.

In the rent-a-car business, for example: What is Hertz's competition? Is it Avis cars? Avis advertising? Avis service? How do other competitors such as Budget, Econocar, and National fit in? What about local rent-a-car firms? Public transportation such as taxis? Buses? Limousines? And where do we fit the high cost of energy and the growing unreliability of automobile service to private individuals?

Uncertainty also exists in relationships with government agencies. Pricing, advertising, and promotion practices are scrutinized by remote agencies populated by people the marketer may never see.

Compared with the marketer's dimly lit world of distant, moving strangers, the world of the manager of other functions is one of real people. They are within the firm. He can see them face to face, talk to them, argue with them. He can discuss their beliefs, motives, and intentions. If a manager uses myths for people, it is not because they are distant, numerous, and inaccessible. Rather it is because he does not know how to create conditions that will enable people in the firm to be psychologically available so he can interact with them as real people.

Uncertainty

There are two major sources of uncertainty for the marketer: (1) the information used for making marketing decisions; (2) the relationship between the firm's actions and what happens in a market.

Decision discretion

Because of many dismal experiences with carefully gathered, irrefutable data, marketers have learned to be skeptical. They do not trust data when making decisions. One need only mention the word "Edsel" to recall a marketing disaster based on data. Marketers use data with caution. They have learned that most marketing data are incomplete, inaccurate, and to some extent irrelevant. The dilemma is that deficiencies in information are rarely evident until after decisions have been made.

To cope with the uncertainty of information, the marketer

views information as a starting point rather than as an end in itself. He uses information as a springboard to create concepts of consumer behavior and product strategy.

Marketers are reluctant to surrender their decision freedom to marketing information. They sense that sometimes relevant information simply does not exist. For example, it is doubtful that surveys in the early 1950s would have uncovered the latent demand for car rentals. The marketer has discovered that consumers frequently do not know what they want until they see tangibly what is available. This creates a decision paradox. A product must be introduced and used by consumers before managers can know whether or not the product is worth introducing.

Competitors add to the uncertainty by constantly devising unpredictable strategies to win fickle consumer preferences. Data may be correct, but by the time it is used it may be about a market that no longer exists because of competitive and consumer changes. Little wonder that marketers differ about how to interpret data.

The meaning of results

The second major source of uncertainty is in the relationship between the firm's actions and the results obtained. When sales volume goes up or down, there usually are many causal factors: prices, advertising, promotion, weather, competitor actions, and so on. Some are under the firm's control, many are not. Determining sensible cause and effect relationships is very difficult.

Managers spend a great deal of time trying to connect market decisions with results. The conclusions often turn out to be sheer fantasy. Consider the following example: A food products company found that sales increased in one of its regional markets. The company's managers concluded that their effort to improve relations with distributors and their institutional advertising were finally taking hold. Many months later a manager discovered that a major competitor had run a promotion in another region, had seriously underestimated demand, and had diverted product shipments to the promotion region. In effect, the company's sales had increased because a major competitor had partially withdrawn from the market.

There are innumerable instances when marketers think a response is a result of what they did, when in fact it had little to do with their actions. Case in point: When sales of bakery products increased, a firm's management attributed the result entirely to their advertising and promotion decisions. Actually a competitor had unknowingly marketed a product that was below his regular quality standard. Consumers had shifted to other brands.

Managers of nonmarketing functions, on the other hand, enjoy relative certainty. In general, they can rely on information. They can make reasonable decisions, given data about the performance of equipment, time required for different tasks, and the productivity of the work force. Managers can also assume stability in relationships. Indeed, it is this dependable fixedness and repetition that enables managers to make reliable cost estimates.

Furthermore, nonmarketing managers can with greater assurance attribute results to their actions. When they change materials or equipment or worker assignments, it is reasonable to attribute changes in output to these actions. There are few additional, inaccessible factors affecting output.

Innovation

Our market economy encourages "innovistic competition." The marketer venerates innovation because it is the most powerful weapon in his arsenal. He uses it to create new demand, to displace competition, and to fight the loss of a market.

Marketers know that innovation is a potent instrument. They use annual style changes in existing products to spring ahead of competitors. In addition, however, they zealously search for new products that will open new markets or decisively sweep old ones.

Most nonmarketing managers want the fruits of innovation

but not its dislocations. They want the increased sales but not the headaches of earning them. Innovation, if it is effective, involves a departure from the known, the traditional, the customary. It disrupts established work methods, reduces efficiency, and raises anxieties. As an abstract concept, innovation is desirable, but when it becomes a tangible change, it arouses strong resistance.

The reward system in many organizations induces conflict among managers who should be collaborating to innovate. For example, in a home products firm, the manufacturing manager was rewarded for increasing production efficiency and reducing costs. He saw his job as saving money, conserving assets, and improving cost effectiveness. As a result he wanted stability. He would fight changes that complicated work and interfered with long production runs.

The marketing manager, on the other hand, was rewarded for increasing sales and profits. He saw his job as spending money, augmenting assets, and improving marketing efficiency. Above all else he wanted innovation. He would fight stability because it interfered with flexibility and rapid responses to changing market opportunities.

In the current language of political images, marketers are revolutionaries, other managers are members of the establishment. When marketers confront other managers one can expect the effects of revolutionary encounter: efforts at containment and suppression from the establishment; efforts at enlargement of protest and increased influence from the revolutionaries.

Consider this case: A firm developed an entirely new concept for a packaged prepared food product. After much laboratory work and pilot manufacturing, the product was successfully test marketed. It subsequently failed when it was placed in a national market. A year later, quite by accident, the marketing manager discovered that manufacturing had decided to deviate from the original specifications for the ingredients. Manufacturing did not want to invest money in new equipment and additional work force to adhere to the close tolerances originally specified for preparing the ingredients. The manufacturing managers disliked the product and had little faith in it from the start. As a result, the product that failed in the national market was significantly inferior to the one that succeeded in the test market.

Social reality

Reality is a social phenomenon to the marketer. It is a relative, changeable matter. If truth exists, it is a social contrivance. Something is true because enough people think it is true. This is neither sinister nor cynical. There is well-known psychological evidence that supports this notion. People will even deny their physical senses when they repeatedly receive contrary information from an authoritative source. In a series of pioneering experiments, it was found that subjects' estimates of the distance a pinpoint of light moved conformed to the estimates they heard reported by other subjects. Actually the light did not move at all. In another series of experiments, it was found that subjects would report that a short line was longer than a long line when they heard all the others in a group report this as their observation. Unknown to the subject, the other members were accomplices of the experimenter.

Marketers expect to influence the way others see the world. This concept is fundamental to their work. They expect to select, arrange, and present facts to highlight a particular impression of reality.

Marketers consider feelings, images, and impressions to be the significant elements of truth. This explains their deep concern about arranging words and information to evoke a particular feeling of reality.

Finally, in the marketer's view, there is no unique solution to problems that involve human beings. There are many good workable solutions.

At the other extreme the nonmarketing manager sees truth as an absolute. This is especially so if he is trained in the hard sciences. In his concept truth exists independently of society. A thing is true (correct) regardless of what people think. Thus, the earth was round even though the prevailing social view at one time was that the earth was flat. That people behaved as if the earth was flat because that was social reality does not concern the nonmarketing manager. Managers, they believe, should use impersonal truths for decisions. Information should not be selected and arranged to create an impression, it should be used only to convey the truth. Finally, they believe there is one best solution—an optimum—in all affairs, and the manager's job is to find it.

Personal commitment

How does the marketer make sense out of his amorphous, shifting world? How does he arrive at a basis for action when there are few external landmarks?

The marketer believes there is only one place he can turn— and that is inward. He has to rely on his impressions, his insights, and his feelings. The first person the marketer must convince is himself. The one person he must continue to convince in the face of inconclusive marketing tests is still himself.

The marketer senses that his personal commitment to a course of action is the critical decision he must make. Often he treats himself as a customer of his own ideas. He believes that if he is not enthusiastic, he surely will be unable to "sell" anyone else. He uses enthusiasm to cope with uncertainty, to overcome inertia and to sweep away resistance to change.

He is both master and victim of his belief in persuasive techniques. He is convinced that other managers will accept his ideas only to the extent that that he creates a favorable image for them. Thus the concern for attractive visual aids and polished presentations.

To the marketer, commitment and enthusiasm are prerequisites of a decision. He believes that if one is dedicated to a plan, ways will surely be found to make it work. In his view there is nothing deadlier than lack of confidence. Half-hearted commitment has in it the seeds of failure.

This is not to say that the marketer does not use analysis. He is an astute analyst. But generally he uses analysis to confirm a decision that he feels is right. Consider this illustration: In an electronics firm a marketing manager was discussing the usefulness of management science in the company with several managers. He summed up his views this way: "We thought highly of the mathematical model developed by the management science people because it provided refined, rational arguments for what we had already decided to do."

The nonmarketing manager has a different style. Because his world is relatively tangible, stable, and measurable, he has a great deal of information to analyze. He starts with the assumption that an action will make no difference or will be a failure. He uses analysis to test this null hypothesis. If analytic methods are inadequate or inconclusive, the nonmarketing manager stays with the nonaction hypothesis. Only after analysis conclusively proves a proposal correct does this manager venture to commit himself.

Since analysis in marketing is often inconclusive, the marketer is frequently frustrated by the noncommital responses of other managers. He finds himself caught in a degenerative process. Not only do other managers not reciprocate his enthusiasm, they become increasingly suspicious of enthusiasm when analysis is inconclusive. The less definitive the analysis, the more commitment and persuasion the marketer feels he must present. As a result, marketers and other managers often find themselves moving farther and farther apart when they try to work under conditions of high uncertainty.

BEHAVIOR NEEDS

What are the implications of these role demands and styles of coping for the marketer as he moves toward top management?

Other points of view

The marketer must accept the fact that other top managers have a significantly different way of looking at business issues. Other managers are internally oriented, expect to deal with real people, are more accustomed to certainty, desire stability, see reality as impersonal and will insist on extensive, conclusive analysis before committing themselves. It is as if marketers and nonmarketers are from two totally different cultures. The potential for conflict between managers from these cultures increases as one moves toward top management where decisions involve greater sums of money and errors are more costly.

The marketer must expect that communication with other managers will get increasingly difficult. Just as he has become an astute marketing executive by using his particular frame of reference, the nonmarketing managers have become astute by using their frame of reference.[1] The marketing manager will often feel that he is not being heard. He is right. But, if it is any consolation, the other managers often feel they are not being heard, and they are also right.

Both types of managers need encouragement to take the other's point of view. Putting oneself in the other's shoes is desirable but very difficult.

In one company marketers and nonmarketers periodically exchange positions. By living as a marketing manager with marketing responsibilities, other managers have a better understanding of the decision dilemmas that face marketers. The marketers also see more clearly the dilemmas of other managers.

Analysis

The marketer can expect an increasing demand for data and analysis that conclusively support his position. Specifically he will be asked to deal with concepts such as subjective probability, computer simulation, and mathematical programming. He will be immersed in examination of discounted cash flows and expected return on investment. To the marketer these forays into the world of quantitative analysis may seem like excessive elaboration of questionable data.

It would be unwise, however, to write off quantitative analysis as futile ritual demanded by small-minded managers. In one firm a marketer who refused to develop minimum skills in quantitative analysis was seen as impulsive and incapable of taking a total corporate point of view. Had he learned some basic analytic concepts he would have been listened to more carefully. He could have more readily obtained meaningful commitment from the other managers.

Freedom to conceptualize

The marketer's contribution to top management will increasingly come in the form of creative insight and conceptual leap. Because this type of contribution is an unsupported departure from conventional ways of thinking, the marketer must expect resistance. There is a need in top management groups for greater support for the discussion of half-formed ideas.

Top management of a machine-tool company operated with an implicit norm that new ideas had to be presented as recommendations that were worked out in complete detail. This mode of operation was useful but it led managers to stick to tried-and-true ideas—ones that they could defend easily. Other, less demanding, norms were occasionally needed to liberate managers to explore innovative ideas.

The marketer can help himself and other managers by developing with them a meeting format that supports the sharing of tentative ideas. The best ideas can be further refined and subjected to careful evaluation later.

Sensitivity to others

The marketer will have to be alert to sense when he becomes aggressively persuasive in support of a concept. Often, he becomes an active *nonlistener*.

A marketing manager in a plastics company tended to interpret the reservations of other managers as momentary anxieties. He treated their objections as an inconvenient lapse in confidence—something he could surmount with additional positive comments. His behavior frustrated and irritated other managers. They felt their views were not being heard as legitimate objections, but were being patronizingly dismissed.

Although marketers often pride themselves on their sensitivity to others, they need as much help as any other manager in seeing their own behavior. There are many programs in individual and group behavior commonly referred to as "laboratory," "sensitivity," or "grid" training that would be valuable for marketers.

Leading the synthesis

Finally, the notion of a systems approach to management is attractive but its implementation depends on behavior that is consistent with the concept. Intellectually, managers can talk about the interests of the total organization. Behaviorally they tend to pursue the interests of their function. To be used successfully in an organization, the systems approach requires a common concept of the boundaries of the system, its parts, the interaction of the parts, and the demands of the environment.

Marketers and other managers often do not share a common concept of the organization as a system. Here is where marketers can and must take initiative. As they move toward top management they should take a leading role in meeting two dilemmas: One is to develop with other managers a shared concept of the business as a system. The second is to design a reward system that pays managers to collaborate to implement the concept. Considering that marketers and other managers are increasingly being trained to see the world in systems concepts, this will be demanding but not insurmountable.

6. Change and Staff Rationality

anagement scientists and operations researchers are staff advisers who use sophisticated, impersonal analysis to solve management problems. Extensively trained in mathematics and economics, they try to follow the precision of the physical sciences. They strive for objectivity, testable hypotheses, and rigorous statistical analysis of data. They represent one leading edge of the knowledge society. Their goal is to use knowledge systematically to increase the rationality of management's decisions.

Increasingly, managers turn to these and other staff specialists for recommendations to help them compete more effectively in volatile markets, reduce costs, and improve return on investment. In some organizations the staff studies policy issues, capital investment proposals, and marketing plans, as a routine input to the decision process.

Staff specialists improve the organization's effectiveness by persuading managers to apply recommendations which usually propose changes to overcome present or anticipated difficulties.

Lack of impact

Expertise in introducing change in a human organization, however, is not necessarily acquired by mastering the rationality of mathematics, finances, or economics. As a matter of fact, management scientists, as well as other staff specialists, are continually concerned about their lack of impact on decisions. Companies are reluctant to provide precise data on their management science successes and failures, and what is obtainable is not easily assessed, but management scientists and managers feel a strong need for improvement.[1] These specialists need a better understanding of how to introduce and implement change, otherwise organizations will get only a fraction of the benefits they offer.

MANAGEMENT SCIENCE VIEWS OF CHANGE

"Doctor-patient" concept

Management scientists' first view of organizational change was similar to the "doctor-patient" concept. The management science staff saw itself as expert, rational, well-intentioned doctors. Managers were seen as patients reacting to symptoms, unable to identify underlying problems, and unskilled in diagnosis. The staff expected that managers would gratefully comply with their expert recommendations. Much to the disappointment of management scientists, there frequently was no change.

The following example is typical of what happened when the staff operated with the doctor-patient concept of change. Over a period of almost 3 years the staff of a large paper-products company developed a sophisticated, interactive information system for the marketers in one division. The marketers could analyze their potential decisions by using terminals connected to a central computer to query a data base with a 10-year history of prices, sales volume, premiums, and so on. They could get statistical information such as averages, correlations, and trends. They could ask "what if" questions using various mathematical models the management scientists had built for different products and markets. The management science staff was pleased with its work.

After the staff considered the system operational, it was turned over to the marketers. Subsequently the system was used so little that within 6 months top management eliminated support from the budget and the terminals were removed. The marketers said the system was of little help. Prices were extremely volatile and the need to react to competitors' short-run marketing tactics was critical. The 10-year history, the statistical routines, and the models had overwhelmed the marketers with data and possibilities. The marketers had originally asked for simple information. The staff had concluded that the marketers did not know what they really needed and gave them massive doses of the latest management science remedies.

Better expertise

Management scientists' second concept of change focused on improving the staff's competence for solving a problem. They believed that change would occur if the staff were more expert and used more sophisticated techniques of analysis. They emphasized defining the problem accurately, using the best mathematical techniques, and finding an optimal solution.[2]

This concept focused on the management scientists and assumed that managers would understand, accept, and implement the staff's rational, but often highly theoretical, solutions. After reviewing disappointing levels of implementation, different observers concluded that, despite scientific rationality, the management scientists were proposing changes with insufficient regard for relevance, timeliness, or acceptance.[3]

Personality differences

Another concept of change proposed by management scientists said that personality differences between managers and management scientists were obstructing change.[4] The key difference supposedly was in their styles of thinking. Managers were pragmatic, concrete, and imprecise in their concepts. On the other hand, management scientists were analytic, abstract, and precise. Theoretically these differences hindered communication and prevented developing the mutual understanding needed for change.

The personality theory of change gained a large following among management scientists. Basically, it reinforced the management scientists' belief that they were rational experts and managers were not. Other than alerting them to possible communication difficulties, the theory did not noticeably improve acceptance of change.

Taking a wide-screen approach, other management scientists searched for factors common to different management science projects.[5] Many factors were identified. For example: support by management, the staff's technical capability, adequacy of resources, and so on. Some or all of these could block change if they were deficient. What was missing was an overall theory that could integrate this large number of variables and tell us how they related to change.

CHANGE AS A SOCIAL PROCESS

Rather than try to make staff specialists more expert or change the personalities of managers, one can adopt a simple, promising approach which views change as a social process[6]—that is, a series of actions and responses determined by the attitudes, beliefs, and decisions of people concerned with the situation. Identifying these forces and understanding how they assist or resist the current state of affairs is the key to change.

The present condition

The first step is to describe the condition we wish to change. For example, it may be an organization's market share, a department's level of inventory, or the turnover of personnel in a section. It may be the output of a plant, the research productivity of a laboratory, or the management process for budgeting capital.

The present condition is a social balance resulting from many aiding and opposing human actions. This social equilibrium is held steady at some average level. If the condition moves away from the average in either direction, human forces push it back. The equilibrium will not change in a lasting way until someone or a group intervenes to alter the balance of forces.

We analyze the current condition to understand the forces— their characteristics, size, and relationships. We can move the system to a new equilibrium level by appropriately changing the pattern of aiding and opposing forces.

The pattern of forces

The forces maintaining the present condition are active and changeable. They are the attitudes, the decisions, and the actions of many people. For example, the level of finished goods inventory results from forces such as consumer attitudes (toward the product's features, price, availability, substitute products); alternative uses of disposable income; management's decisions; and competitor's decisions (regarding product design, pricing, promotion, and distribution).

Consider this illustration: In 1979 Chrysler Corporation had a large inventory of unused, finished cars. The lack of cash flow threatened the solvency of the company and prompted an appeal to the government for loan guarantees of up to $1 billion. The loan guarantee would have had little effect on the inventory. The forces maintaining the inventory included consumer attitudes toward Chrysler products, the increasing share of disposable income going to pay for energy, General Motors' introduction of small, front-wheel-drive cars, and so on. The inventory equilibrium would not have changed if several key forces had not been changed while others stayed the same: Chrysler management offered a $400 rebate on the purchase of many slow-moving models; consumer attitudes shifted in favor of Chrysler products; competitors did not match Chrysler's rebate offer.

The forces are affected by people working, communicating,

and interacting. These "social" activities change attitudes, decisions, and actions.

Staff pressure increases opposition

In its desire to change management's decisions, the staff sometimes tries to overcome managerial resistance by forcing its position. For example, staff may persuade higher management to direct lower levels to implement staff conclusions. Usually such actions increase the operating manager's opposition. The net result is no change but greater tension between staff and management than before.

Staff can pressure, threaten, or indirectly attack managers in many ways. But managers have equal or greater power and total control of the implementation of staff recommendations. Managers can postpone, block, or subvert staff-imposed directives. Unfortunately, even though staff and managers have common interests, the staff's approach to change can provoke a stalemate under increasing tension.

Generally, it is better for staff to work on reducing rather than overwhelming opposing forces. Then, without forcing, the present equilibrium will move without increasing tension. But, this approach means staff must be able to understand and competently diagnose social forces. Also, staff must have skill in helping managers explore their resistance without arousing defensiveness.

PHASES OF CHANGE

Change has three phases: (1) unfreezing—increasing the receptivity of others to a possible change in the distribution or size of social forces; (2) moving—altering the number, direction, or size of aiding and opposing forces, thereby shifting to a new level of equilibrium; and (3) refreezing—stabilizing and maintaining the new equilibrium. Each of the three phases consists of supporting activities which we shall now examine.[7]

Unfreezing

Unfreezing depends on disconfirmation and psychological support. Disconfirmation is information that tells you your behavior is ineffective, or not as effective as it could be. It is feedback that alerts you to a need for change, increases your receptivity to alternatives, and stimulates search. Without disconfirmation we tend to assume we are doing well and there is no need to change. The old saying, "Things may have to get worse before they can get better," recognizes the importance of disconfirmation.

Disconfirming feedback takes different forms: (1) *objective measures* that show your intended level of performance was not achieved—for example, your unit did not meet its sales goal or its return on investment; (2) *social comparison* that shows your performance is inferior to a comparable unit—for example, sales in your region or store are below those of comparable regions or stores, or the cost efficiency of your plant is below that of comparable plants; (3) *appraisals* by other important persons, such as superior, peers, or subordinates, that indicate you are not attaining intended results—for example, your style of management does not stimulate the dedication, loyalty, and motivation you need in coworkers, or your marketing program is not inducing the commitment or motivation you need in dealers in your distribution system; (4) *criticism* from other important persons that indicates your performance is deficient compared with some *highly valued ideal.* For example, your decisions are criticized for consistently discriminating against one group of employees.

Psychological support means management creates a climate that leads others to feel that ineffectiveness is undesirable and can be remedied, that facing up to ineffectiveness is, in the long run, more useful and satisfying than denying it. Psychological support provides assurance that change is possible. It develops confidence that you and others have the mental and physical ability to surmount difficulties.

Both disconfirmation and psychological support are needed for unfreezing. Some organizations provide substantial disconfirmation but little psychological support. They arouse resistance, fear, and stress along with awareness of a need for change but do not instill confidence that change can be accomplished successfully. Other organizations provide psychological support but little disconfirmation. They induce loyalty and willingness to change but leave people confused and groping regarding what to change.

Moving

Moving blends two approaches to problem solving: One is objective and impersonal; the second is social and personal.

The impersonal approach conceptualizes a problem by assuming that people are not a significant causal factor and those who will be affected by a solution need not be considered. It is an objective, disciplined approach which defines criteria for a preferred solution, develops alternatives, and chooses a course of action.

Management science staffs are primarily trained in this approach. They depersonalize a situation and transform it into abstract variables largely devoid of human content. For example, one study of the effectiveness of missionary salespeople considered each prospect's past orders, the frequency of sales calls, the time since the last call, and the total compensation and expenses of the sales force. From this model, recommendations were made regarding the optimal frequency of calls and the minimum and maximum period between calls.

The model did not consider such personal, human variables as whom the salesperson spoke to, what they spoke about, and the quality of their relationship. The impersonal approach assumed that the sales force was competent and well trained. Therefore, it assumed that over a large number of calls each salesperson spoke to the right prospects, about the right topics, and developed a good relationship. If this assumption was incorrect, the model and the recommendations would have been deficient and potentially misleading.

The social approach to moving considers who is involved in

each stage of problem solving. It considers who defines the problem, establishes criteria, develops alternatives, and selects a solution. It also considers how they are involved.

The management science staff has many choices in regard to who is involved. It may consult top management, managers of the unit being studied, and workers. In addition, it may consult union representatives, customers, other staff groups, external consultants, and so on. It is possible that the staff involves all, some, or none of these in different stages.

Extensive Consultation. When others are involved in moving there are many possibilities as to how they are involved. For example, the staff may continuously consult the manager in each stage of problem solving. The staff and the manager could share, discuss, and adjust their thinking and models on the basis of these consultations. Each could provide inputs and evaluations to the other. Each would be free to originate questions or express concerns to the other.

The staff and the manager may test various proposals by applying them in a limited area. They can make adjustments based on the results and repeat testing until they arrive at a satisfactory solution. In such an approach they make sequential, step-by-step improvements.

Limited Consultation. In contrast, at the other extreme, the staff may ask managers to provide data and nothing more. The staff then analyses the data and tests solutions alone. When it is through, the staff reports its recommendations to top management, which decides what to do next.

When top management believes that a drastic change is needed and that time is limited and consulting others will arouse prolonged, increasing opposition, then it often directs the staff to use this nonconsultation approach. The staff studies the situation and submits its recommendations. Top management implements the solution and deals with the opposition and human repercussions afterward. This method of moving is called the "great leap."

For example, this method was used to reorganize the paperwork operations of a large bank. Staff minimally consulted unit managers and designed a major reorganization. Previously operations for all customers had been centralized in one massive unit. Under the new organization, self-contained, complete service units were formed for each of four different customer groups. Equipment was moved to the new configuration during one weekend. Then, management spent the next 2 to 3 years getting the system to work as intended and dealing with the aftermath of severe human difficulties.

Sometimes, however, the staff follows nonconsultation without being directed to by top management. Staff may believe that a major change is needed, but with nonconsultation there is little probability it will be accepted by unit managers or top management.

It is important that staff recognize that moving requires more than an optimal solution to an impersonally formulated problem. Organizations are social systems and moving requires an effective combination of both the impersonal and the social factors.

Refreezing

Refreezing occurs through confirmation, psychological support, and self-management. Confirmation is feedback that your performance is effective. It comes from several sources, such as objective measurements, responses of others that verify you are at a new level of effectiveness, comparison showing that your performance equals or exceeds that of another comparable unit, or from your own observation that you have come closer to attaining some ideal level of performance. Confirmation also comes through rewards from others. These include increased salary, bonuses, promotion, and greater responsibility.

Psychological support in refreezing means management creates a climate that leads you to feel satisfaction and pleasure with the new behavior. It is encouragement to practice and use the new behavior. It is accepting occasional error as normal and not being diverted into hastily abandoning the new behavior at the first sign of difficulty. It is repeating the new behavior until it is more familiar and comfortable than prior behavior.

Self-management occurs when superiors transfer monitoring and control of the new behavior to you. They no longer need to oversee your behavior but rely on your self-control. Finally, management shows confidence in your self-management when it asks you to guide others who have been directed to adopt the change.

A STUDY OF
MANAGEMENT SCIENTISTS

The three-phase concept of change was used to study the success and failure experiences of a large group of management scientists.[8] First, 11 expert, widely experienced management scientists, identified by the officers of a professional society of management scientists, agreed to participate in the initial stage of the study. In a tape-recorded interview, lasting from 2 to 4 hours, each management scientist was asked to select and discuss two critical incidents—that is, two significant change projects from his personal experience, one exceptionally successful and one exceptionally unsuccessful.

The interviews were analyzed for items relating to the three phases of change and the measurement of success. After refinement and pilot testing, a 64-item questionnaire was developed. Then 154 management scientists, out of 391 members of the Institute of Management Science, a leading society in the field, answered the questionnaire. They provided data on 140 successful and 140 unsuccessful change projects.

Results

The study confirmed that successful change could be explained by the three-phase, social-process concept of unfreezing, moving, refreezing. In successful projects, favorable forces in each phase correlated significantly with successful outcomes. In unsuccessful projects, unfavorable forces in each phase correlated significantly with unsuccessful outcomes.

Also, success in the early phases helped the later phases. For example, unfreezing helped moving, and moving helped refreezing. But failure in an early phase decreased the chances of success in a later phase. Failure to unfreeze triggered opposition to moving. Failure to move aroused resistance to refreezing.

The favorable and unfavorable forces in each phase consisted of specific attitudes, decisions, and actions of top managers, unit managers, and management scientists. These forces are summarized in Table 6-1 and will be discussed below.

Table 6-1   Forces in Unfreezing, Moving, and Refreezing

Favorable	Unfavorable
Unfreezing	
1. Top and unit managers felt the problem was important to company.	1. Unit managers could not state their problems clearly.
2. Top managers became involved.	2. Top managers felt the problem was too big.
3. Unit managers recognized a need for change.	3. Unit managers did not recognize need for change.
4. Top managers initiated the study.	4. Unit managers felt threatened by the project.
5. Top and unit managers were open, candid.	5. Unit managers resented the study.
6. Unit managers revised some of their assumptions.	6. Unit managers lacked confidence in the management scientists.
	7. Unit managers felt they could do the study alone.
Moving	
1. Unit managers and management scientists gathered data jointly.	1. Management scientists could not educate the unit managers.
2. Relevant data were accessible, available.	2. Needed data were not made available.
3. New alternatives were devised.	3. Unit managers did not help develop a solution.
4. Unit managers reviewed and evaluated alternatives.	4. Unit managers did not understand

5. Top managers were advised of options.
6. Top managers helped develop a solution.
7. Proposals were improved sequentially.

Refreezing

1. Unit managers tried the solution.
2. Utilization showed the superiority of the new solution.
3. Management scientists initiated positive feedback after early use.
4. Solution was widely accepted after initial success.
5. Unit managers were satisfied.
6. Solution was used in other areas.
7. The change improved the performance of the unit.

the solution of the management scientists.
5. Management scientists felt the study was concluded too quickly.

1. Management scientists did not try to support new managerial behavior after the solution was used.
2. Management scientists did not try to reestablish stability after the solution was used.
3. Results were difficult to measure.
4. Standards for evaluating results were lacking.
5. Top managers ignored the solution recommended by the management scientists.
6. Solution incompatible with the needs and resources of the unit.
7. Top managers did not encourage other units to use the solution.

Unfreezing

The data showed that unfreezing is a complex, unstable phase. During unfreezing, management scientists, top managers, and unit managers separately attempt to identify the problem, assess its severity, and estimate the need for change.

Different managers describe the problem differently. Some may have difficulty stating the problem clearly or succinctly so their initial statements are vague or ambiguous.

Managers differ about the focus and scope of the problem. Some see it as narrow and well defined—for example, maintaining adequate inventory of a particular product. Others see the problem more broadly. For example, they consider the inventory condition to be only a symptom. For them the real problems are improper marketing policies, deficient purchasing, and poor manufacturing practices all of which are inadequately integrated.

During unfreezing, different managers attribute different degrees of importance to the problem. Some consider it crucial. Others consider it of minor importance. Sometimes the staff thinks the problem is important but managers do not. In some instances top managers and staff feel there is a need for change, but the unit managers do not. In other instances unit managers feel a need for change, but top management or staff do not.

Amid these differences, the staff, the top management, and the unit managers negotiate a relationship that may or may not be productive. If they have similar perceptions of the problem, similar estimates of its importance, and if management is open, then they develop a productive three-party alliance. But if top managers and unit managers differ substantially about the problem or its importance, then the management science staff may be drawn into the conflict.

The staff usually prefers to see itself as impartial and objective, but in a dispute managers see the staff as an ally or opponent, depending upon whose views it supports. The implication is that the rational management scientist cannot focus exclusively on an impersonal analysis of problems. If he ignores the social forces in the unfreezing phase, his efforts to get a solution implemented later may be futile.

The management scientists must help prepare the organization for change from the outset. When he negotiates his relationship in a project, he will get many clues about the condition of unfreezing in the attitudes, decisions, and actions of different managers. He should pay close attention, otherwise he may be trapped and whipsawed in a conflict between top managers and unit managers.

Moving

Moving depends on unfreezing, and the two phases overlap substantially. The management scientist should carefully listen to the concerns of unit and top managers during unfreezing. If he ignores them and then tries to proceed, or if they believe he does not understand, then moving will be difficult and resisted. The unit will withhold relevant data and its managers will not help develop practical solutions. As a result, managers will not understand or accept the staff's proposals. During unfreezing, if unit managers see management scientists as adversaries, they act out their resistance during the moving phase.

On the other hand, if unit managers accept the need for change during unfreezing, their favorable attitudes help moving. Also, if top and unit managers have similar concepts of the problem, they avoid skirmishing and sniping, and moving is easier. Finally, if managers and management scientists develop trust in each other during unfreezing, they analyze underlying issues and constructively consider each other's proposals during moving.

In a successful moving phase, managers and management scientists communicate openly and continuously. They gather relevant data together. Managers periodically and nondefensively review proposed alternatives. The staff adjusts and improves proposals on the basis of the interim reviews. Managers and staff regularly inform top management of progress and top managers make critical policy inputs while alternatives are fluid. For example, they identify alternatives that will be unacceptable for qualitative reasons such as unsatisfactory impact on suppliers or employees. Such judgments are the province of top management and successful moving incorporates them while solutions are being shaped.

Refreezing

Refreezing overlaps and depends on moving. It is important to recognize that a change is not successfully completed simply by moving, although many management science staff specialists think it is. They believe that when managers agree to a solution they have nothing more to do. Unfortunately, they overlook the important task of refreezing.

In successful refreezing, the managers and management science staff carefully test solutions and evaluate results together. Management scientists give supportive feedback to the managers who helped design and implement the solution by letting them know that the time they invested and the risks they took were worthwhile. Managers and staff help each other sustain the change through the misunderstandings, mistakes, and decreased performance that frequently occur during the early stages of implementing a change.

Successful refreezing depends on evidence of effective application and timely reports of superior results. The managers and the staff should plan the gathering of relevant data and the design of reports. They should not leave these information activities to the existing reporting system or chance.

In successful refreezing, even after managers apply the solution, top managers and management scientists give them positive feedback to encourage them to continue to use and improve the solution. Finally, with the first unit serving as a model and giving guidance, management introduces the solution in other units.

In contrast, during unsuccessful refreezing, top managers ignore or disapprove the staff's recommendations. Even after a solution has been applied successfully in one unit, top management signals disapproval by not encouraging other units to use it.

Managers and management science staff move away from each other in unsuccessful refreezing. The staff does little to assist implementation because it lacks either interest or understanding.

Refreezing was also unsuccessful if the staff's recommendations went far beyond the needs of the unit. The staff's solution might be an ideal, ultimate solution, but when managers felt the changes were more sweeping than was necessary or acceptable, the entire solution was dropped.

If managers and staff did not define standards for evaluating results, refreezing was not likely to be successful. If outcomes were hard to measure and managers and staff did not devise substitute measures, refreezing suffered.

Finally, if the preceding moving phase was unsuccessful with the unit managers but top management nevertheless directed the unit to implement the staff's recommendations, unit managers resented the staff and resisted its influence on implementation.

Circularity

Successful outcomes support refreezing and refreezing helps reproduce successful outcomes. Therefore, feedback about successful outcomes is crucial. It helps stabilize new behavior and leads to self-motivated repetition.

New behavior may be more effective than past behavior, but if there is no refreezing, it attenuates and disappears. The management science staff must understand that systematic reporting, psychological support, and rewards are essential to stabilizing change.

The balance of forces

It would be erroneous to conclude that there are only favorable forces in successful changes. It would be equally incorrect to assume that there are only unfavorable forces in unsuccessful changes. Both favorable and unfavorable forces are present in each phase of change in all projects. In successful projects, however, the number and size of favorable forces is greater in each phase than the unfavorable forces. Managers and staff identify and reduce the opposing forces and enhance the aiding forces. It is the net balance of forces that determines change.

Application to other projects

In this instance the three-phase, social-process concept of change was used to study the change efforts of a specific group of staff specialists—management scientists. The methods and conclusions, however, apply to the change efforts of other staff specialists such as financial analysts, marketing analysts, industrial engineers, and so on because the forces in each phase of a management science project are usually found in most other change projects. By systematically identifying the favorable and unfavorable forces (summarized in Table 6-1) and evaluating their net balance in each phase, a manager and his staff can assess the probability of a successful change. They can also see which phase they are in and what they can do to facilitate change.

7. Policy and the General Manager

ne critical source of knowledge is an understanding of how your organization formulates policies. Most managers and planners agree that periodic review of the policy formulation process would help generate better policies. Just as an artist steps back from his canvas and reexamines his work from a different perspective, so managers and planners believe it is useful to pause regularly to analyze the policy formulation process. The benefits can be substantial.

For example, a new president of a company in metals and chemicals initiated a review of the policy process 1 year after he took office. His predecessor, a man of strong views, had been president for 10 years. In response to the question, "Who is presently involved in the policy process?" the study found that a marketing manager of a key product expected to grow in sales had minimal participation. Apparently there had been differences with the prior president. He had reorganized the company and in effect excluded this and several other marketing managers from the policy process.

Based on the study, the marketing manager of the key product and several other managers were again actively consulted in the policy process. As a result, the company's plan to expand capacity to make and sell the key product was significantly changed. The marketing manager's assessments and judgments, which previously had received minor attention, became direct inputs to policy deliberations. He correctly estimated that two major customers who purchased 30 percent of the key product were committed to building capacity within the next 3 years to make most if not all of what they were buying. Moreover, those two customers represented a trend which could significantly alter the structure of the market. Had the company gone ahead with its previous strategy it would have had excess capacity in a market that was facing declining prices. The example is one of many illustrating the growing interest in reviewing the policy process.

MODELS FOR ANALYZING THE POLICY PROCESS

Two developments have sparked efforts to give the policy process the careful review it deserves. First, earlier, simple notions of the policy process are being replaced by more comprehensive models which do a better job of telling us what questions to ask and where to look. Second, whereas in the past a review could easily arouse defensiveness and resistance, we are beginning to understand more clearly what factors lead to creative, constructive use of a review.

There are three types of models of the policy process. The first two are comparatively simple; the third is complex. The first type is called *actor models* because it focuses on the general manager as the main character in the drama of policy formulation. The second type is called *procedure models* because it concentrates on defining steps and schedules which together should result in a logical, tightly knit formal planning process. The third type is called a *problem-solving model*. It subsumes the first two and will be discussed in detail. It looks at policy formulation as a specific instance of the class of problems called genuine decisions and then analyzes the steps needed to solve such problems.

Finally, as most managers know from personal experience, it is one thing to have a model and another to apply it successfully in an organization. Therefore, we shall discuss factors leading to constructive use of a review; for example, the concepts and attitudes of the general manager, the organization's recent profitability, and other elements.

ACTOR MODELS

Rational architect

Actor models spotlight the general manger who, as the formal leader of the organization, has tremendous influence on policy decisions. One model, which we shall call the rational architect, casts the general manager as the principle and possibly the sole architect of strategy.[1] Given his centrality and influence, this model concludes that it is the general manager's problem-solving and synthesizing abilities which lead to effective policies. The model asserts, therefore, that the person selected to be general manager should be highly rational and dedicated. Advocates cite as supporting evidence cases of outstanding, rational individuals such as Robert MacNamara who led the Ford Motor Company to profitable operations then became Secretary of Defense and subsequently president of the World Bank.

Persuasive prophet

This actor model not only defines the general manager as the principal architect of policy but also requires that he have the vision to see the need for a major change in strategy and the ability to overcome his subordinates' ignorance and persuade them to his views. Advocates support the model by citing a successful turnaround such as George Romney's redirection of American Motors to small cars in the 1960s, which was a major break with the historic practices of the automotive "majors." "Seven years and the departure of a number of top officials were required to effect this change."[2]

Research indicates, however, that a significant number of

managers are not objective or prophetic, have difficulty taking a long-term view, and select policies which fit their personal background and interests.[3] True, the policy decisions of one outstanding general manager thinking and acting alone may be extremely effective, but over a large sample of general managers, a process consisting mainly of his private deliberations and conclusions is likely to permit distortions which lead to deficient policies.

Fallible opportunist

To offset deficiencies of the first two models, a fallible-opportunist model has been developed. The model is based on the premise that safeguards such as discussion and review must be built into a general-manager–centered process. It takes into account the serious possibility that the general manager acting alone will tend to underestimate risks and overlook negative side effects. Also, the model points out that a manager, after attaining power, may attempt to preserve his position by formulating policies which further his personal ambitions rather than the interests of the organization.[4] Thus, unless there are safeguards, this model cautions that a general-manager–centered process may deliberately or unwittingly go astray.

Advocates of the fallible-opportunist model support their case by citing a serious failure. For example, General Dynamics' foray into building commercial jet aircraft under the leadership of a hard-driving, visionary general manager, brought the company to the brink of bankruptcy. High development and production costs, low sales volume, and fixed-price contracts led to losses of over $400 million. For years, several levels of the organization knew that their plane would cost many times the original estimate, pricing it out of the market. Also, delivery would be 1 to 2 years later than target, making its entry so late that most airlines would have purchased planes from competitors. The company's policy process was unable to reconcile this critical information with the general manager's vision, so it was suppressed.

PROCEDURE MODELS

Procedure models conceptualize policy formulation as a repetitive process.[5] There is a cycle of activities such as establishing corporate objectives, defining division goals and plans, delineating supporting functional plans, and developing capital and operating budgets. Proposals are developed at one organizational level, transmitted to other levels, and then revised in cross-level negotiations.

Procedure models, in contrast to actor models, see the *corporate* general manager as an overseer, reviewer, and approver who resolves cross-level conflicts. The *division* general manager, on the other hand, often retains some qualities of the principal architect of strategy for his division, but procedure models imply that he is one of many actors in a scheme of activities, roles, and organization levels.

Compared with actor models, procedure models are more complex and richer in suggesting ways to improve the policy process. Actor models basically say: Select a qualified general manager and put safeguards around him. If policies are deficient, replace him. Procedure models, however, assume that the general manager is reasonably qualified and focus on systematic performance of a series of steps in a repetitive planning cycle.

A PROBLEM-SOLVING MODEL

Managers and planners accept the general manager as a key actor in policy formulation. They also accept procedure models as a guide to designing and scheduling steps in the policy process. But they sense that policy making in a turbulent environment requires more than a competent general manager and systematic procedures. That additional element, which often remains unfocused and unexamined, is *a process which mobilizes analytic ability, asks probing questions, and stimulates creative insight.*

The purpose here is to supplement the actor and the procedure models with a problem-solving model which extends our concept of the policy process. The problem-solving model consists of nine interdependent activities (see Figure 7-1).[6] We will discuss several of the activities, introduce illustrations and cases along the way, and pose questions which the manager or planner can use to analyze his organization's policy process.

First, we will briefly discuss the notion of genuine decision behavior to clarify when an organization ought to use a system as comprehensive as the model. Second, we will describe the nonlinear character of the problem-solving model. Then we will analyze the different activities which make up the model.

Genuine decision behavior

Policy formulation is a particular case of a more general activity called genuine decision behavior.[7] A genuine decision involves a substantial commitment of resources, has significant, long-lasting consequences, inflicts severe penalities if erroneous, and is extremely difficult, if not impossible, to reverse. Thus, policy decisions affect the survival and long-term welfare of an organization, whereas other decisions, at worst, involve minor setbacks. President Kennedy's comment about the difference between his approach to domestic problems compared with foreign affairs illustrates a grim awareness of genuine decision behavior. "The big difference," he said, "is between a bill being defeated and the country being wiped out."[8]

Policy formulation, therefore, should activate the full scope of management's problem-solving responses. It should initiate *managerial questioning of expectations and assumptions*. It should trigger a *review of goals and values*. It should stimulate *creativity in generating alternatives and formulating criteria of evaluation*.

Nonlinear process

Logic suggests that orderly problem solving should follow the sequence of elements listed in Figure 7-1. Studies of complex problem solving, however, indicate that flashes of insight, or

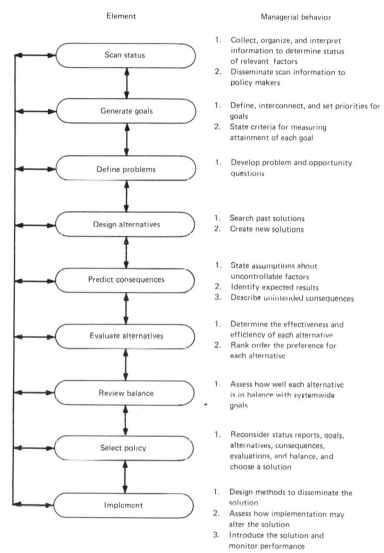

Figure 7-1. A problem-solving model of the policy process.

seeing the problem in a new "gestalt," usually occur after first solution attempts fail but at no special stage in the process. To show that management policy behavior may iterate through loops and subloops until it generates an acceptable policy, double-headed arrows connect each activity to all the others. Thus in contrast to procedure models, the problem-solving model recognizes the need for subcycles complementing the formal planning schedule.

Increasing the capacity to contribute proposals

One question suggested by the problem-solving model is: How does the formal planning procedure affect managerial contributions to policy formulation? It appears that a manager's freedom to depart occasionally from standard procedures may increase his capacity to contribute alternatives and elevate the creativity of policies.

Policy formation has been described as a process in which middle managers propose policy recommendations and top executives develop corporate strategy based on those recommendations.[9] A large research and development company found, however, that middle management's ability to contribute policy recommendations depended on its freedom to depart from formal planning and review procedures. Vice-presidents and their subordinates in the company were required to submit annual budget projections, quarterly revisions with detailed explanations of deviations, and monthly reviews of technical progress. These demanding formal procedures were useful for controlling current operations but left the managers with little time and scant information for recommending meaningful, let alone creative, longer-term policies.

In response to the president's complaint that he was getting few policy contributions from his subordinates, data were gathered on man-hours at each level of management devoted to reports and reviews of current operations in contrast to the policy activities in the problem-solving model. The results showed heavy involvement of middle and upper management in reviews of current operations far beyond the most extreme estimate of the president. Time devoted to policy planning, in contrast, was far below his estimate. The extreme imbalance shown by the data triggered a thorough review of the policy process. Over a period of 18 months, most review of current operations was delegated to lower levels and the policy process was substantially revised.

Nine months after the process revision, the company instituted a major change in organization structure based on a new strategy to meet its 10-year forecast of environmental and technical trends. After the new structure had been in place 6 years, management still considered it a good fit to the environment.

Now, let us look at several key elements in reviewing the policy process.

SCAN STATUS

The policy process begins with a scan of the environment and the organization to locate problems and opportunities. Scan data must be collected, organized, and disseminated. What data are collected and what is overlooked or ignored is a critical determinant of what threats and opportunities managers and planners will see, if any.[10] The problem-solving model calls our attention to a simple question which organizations often find difficult to answer: "What is the present system for scanning status?"   ·

Reviewing the scan activity

In an effort to answer the question systematically, managers and planners in one organization operating in an especially complex environment began by preparing a list of items they believed should go into a scan of the environment and the organization. This exercise itself was informative because of the great variety of views different managers and planners expressed.

The list was circulated to several levels of management. Each manager and planner was asked to identify those items for which he felt he was a qualified source of information. In addition, if the person did not consider himself a qualified source, he was asked who inside or outside the organization was. A sample of the managers and planners were subsequently interviewed in depth to clarify and add perspective to the written responses.

The results indicated that functional managers generally considered themselves a qualified source of short-term information (2 years or less) about their function. But they felt much less qualified beyond that time horizon and stated that additional sources should be used. The financial accounting function was seen as the primary source of information on the current status of the organization. Planners were seen as the primary source in the organization for information on general economic conditions. Sources for trends in government activities, competitor behavior, consumer interests, and supplier patterns were vague and diffuse. Many managers and planners read the same trade journals and trade association bulletins which made for consistency in their scan image content and also consistency in their gaps.

A management review of the scan system revealed misunderstanding about the quality and reliability of several information sources. What had been thought to be reliable assumptions regarding several critical items were found to be more a matter of substantial redundancy from using a small number of common sources. In addition, important information gaps were identified.

A new design for scanning

Managers and planners then formed a task force which recommended improvements to the scanning system. In the final outcome, scan information needs were divided into categories such as markets, technology, competitors, and so on with detailed components listed in each. Then responsibility for reporting on each category was assigned to a primary and a secondary independent group of managers and planners. This somewhat elaborate system assured that each category would be covered and conflicting views would be heard. Managers and planners were encouraged to communicate important data outside their assignment to those responsible for the category. A scan information integrating group was formed to synthesize the reports from the category groups.

This, of course, is not the only approach to scanning, but it is the one this organization felt was best for its needs in a complex, rapidly changing environment. Management's review of its policy process, using the problem-solving model proposed here, stimulated increased awareness and understanding of scanning and facilitated major changes in how scanning was done.

There are many other questions the model can suggest about scanning. We present a few examples without discussion. For instance: What is the form of the outputs of the scan system? How are they used? How, if at all, does the scan system incorporate crucial qualitative information? Which managers get which outputs of the scan system? Why? Who monitors and reviews the scan system? How?

GENERATE GOALS

Managers with the aid of planners should generate an array of goals and formulate criteria for measuring attainment of each goal. They should evaluate the difference between the array of goals and the scan of status, setting aside inconsequential gaps and concentrating on the significant threats and opportunities.

The problem-solving model indicates that managers and planners must be alert to the need to change goals and must anticipate how changes in some goals will impact other goals. They should examine how goal priorities and related costs change over time. They should analyze strategic goals to determine when they do not reinforce one another but overlap, are contradictory, or omit important areas.

Since goals are central to the policy process a review should examine how the system generates goals and deals with differing views of goals. The model suggests these questions: (1) What array of goals is perceived by different managers? (2) How do these differences affect policy formulation and implementation? (3) How are goals examined for contradictions, overlap, and omissions? Here relations among divisions and between divisions and corporate headquarters become especially important.

Goal gaps

In the case of a large, multidivision firm, for example, each division was treated as an independent business. Each division faced significant competition from 6 to 25 firms in its markets. Each division had defined its primary mission as growth in the sense of increasing dollar and unit sales. Corporate managers and planners went out of their way to avoid interfering with division strategies and operations. The effect over a period of years was growth in sales volume across most divisions but flat and occasionally declining profits. Corporate financial resources were heavily strained to support the growth. Long-term debt had increased significantly, additional shares had been sold, and earnings per share were down. Cash resources had declined substantially and the firm was borrowing short-term funds extensively from banks.

After reviewing corporate performance, under the direction of a new general manager, a task force of managers, planners, and consultants concluded that the policy process inadequately analyzed and synthesized division goals. Corporate management decided that it would have to institute a more rigorous process of defining and analyzing division goals. It would also have to examine division goals more thoroughly for consistency, gaps, and interactions with each other and with corporate strategy.

A change in generating goals

The general manager expected the change would be painful, given the history of division autonomy. He proceeded, nevertheless, by first substantially raising the competence of the corporate planning and control activities through small increases in personnel and selective replacements. He also formed a strategy discussion group composed of corporate managers and planners. Within 1 year he had a good understanding of the strategy, issues, and situation in each division. The divisions were then realigned into clusters of related businesses, and group vice-presidents were installed. Then he formed a strategy council composed of the group vice presidents and selected corporate managers and planners.

The policy planning process became more systematic with a defined cycle of reports, reviews, commentaries, negotiations, and approved plans. Much greater attention was devoted to generating and analyzing goals. As one would expect, many questions were raised about the corporation's concept of growth. Which divisions should grow and which should not? Why? Which businesses should it be in? Which should it not be in?

The outcome was definition of a wide range of different rates of growth for different divisions. For the first time, divestment possibilities were analyzed regularly. The firm has since divested two major unprofitable divisions and withdrawn from several other unprofitable businesses. Several division businesses were found to have much greater growth and profit potential than had been realized. These were given additional resources and did extremely well. Overall, total sales have grown moderately but profits have improved substantially and debt is no longer a problem.

DEFINE PROBLEMS
AND OPPORTUNITIES

Well-framed, penetrating questions are essential to the definition of problems and opportunities. Managers and planners should probe assumptions, identify uncertainties, and examine relations among critical factors.

The model suggests these questions: (1) What is the process

for defining problems and opportunities? (2) Who is asking policy questions? How well do those questions stimulate creative
search? (3) How are managers who ask penetrating questions
treated?

Penetrating inquiry:
Disturbing but necessary

The following example illustrates one use of questions in ferreting out problems and opportunities in a complex political setting. In *Corridors of Power,* C. P. Snow's fictional account of England's struggle to formulate a policy for nuclear weapons during
the late 1950s, a member of parliament assigned to the Ministry
of Defense makes the following statement to an informal gathering of arms manufacturers, military personnel, and members of
parliament:

> I'm going to ask the questions. As I say, no one knows the
> answers. But if all of us think about them, we may be able to say
> something that decent people, of good will all over the world, are
> waiting to hear. First, if there is no agreement or control, how
> many countries are going to possess thermo-nuclear weapons by,
> say, 1967. My guess, and this is a political guess, and yours is as
> good as mine is that four or five will actually have them. Unless it
> is not beyond the wit of man to stop them. Second, does this
> spread of weapons make thermo-nuclear war more or less likely?
> Again your guess is as good as mine. But mine is sombre. Third,
> why are countries going to possess themselves of these weapons?
> Is it for national security, or for less rational reasons? Fourth, can
> this catastrophe—no, that is going further than I feel inclined; I
> ought to say, this extreme increase of danger—can it be stopped?
> Is it possible that any of us, any country or group of countries can
> give a message or indication that will, in fact, make military and
> human sense?[11]

The questions were disturbing and the penetrating inquiry
aroused strong antagonism. The policy maker's dilemma was that
he would jeopardize his career by asking probing questions, but
if he did not, who would? His policy recommendations were

subsequently adopted, but he was undermined by opponents who resented his searching inquiry. He was not reelected.

DESIGN ALTERNATIVES

Managers and planners design alternatives by first searching past policies for a solution to current dilemmas. If this fails, they must go beyond familiar policies and invent new solutions. The problem-solving model suggests that management review how the policy process stimulates the design of creative alternatives.

The creative leap

Consider the following example from Alfred Sloan's chronicle of General Motors.[12] Sales by all manufacturers of cars in the low-price range had grown from 52 percent of the industry's total in 1926 to 73 percent in 1933. If General Motors continued with its existing product-market policies, it would have four lines—Pontiac, Oldsmobile, Buick, Cadillac—in the high-price group which had declined to 27 percent of the market. On the other hand, there was only one line—Chevrolet—in 73 percent of the market.

In 1933, Donaldson Brown, General Motors' chief financial officer, proposed to reduce operating costs by eliminating two divisions in the high-price group, cutting back to a total of three. This was an alternative based on past policies. Mr. Sloan, however, favored retaining all five divisions despite the extra cost. He had in mind a new alternative which imaginatively departed from the past.

If General Motors had followed its traditional policy, it would have increased its coverage in the low-price market by establishing more Chevrolet dealers, who, having the same product, would compete directly with each other. Instead, Mr. Sloan proposed increasing the product line variety of the traditional high-price group to overlap the low-price group. That creative alternative subsequently became company policy. It is instructive that the General Motors' policy process permitted examination of such an unusual alternative at a time when the economy was in the depth of a depression.

Managerial imagination still needed

Another question the problem-solving model calls to our attention is: How may quantitative methods of analysis affect the design of creative policy alternatives?

Advances in mathematical and computer-based analysis are increasingly helpful in evaluating policy alternatives. Managers must be aware, however, that these sophisticated tools of a knowledge society primarily identify poor alternatives which should be discarded. They do not create new alternatives. Mathematical models and computers have great value but they do not diminish the manager's and planner's responsibility to think imaginatively. In the case of General Motors' product-market dilemma in 1933, today's sophisticated quantitative techniques would have helped Donaldson Brown identify which two divisions should have been eliminated. They would not, however, have created Mr. Sloan's imaginative alternative.

REVIEW BALANCE

After policies have been generated, evaluated, and ranked, they should be reviewed for overall balance. Up to this point each proposal has been examined against criteria and conditions specific to its class of proposals. For example, a proposal to expand capacity falls into a class of proposals concerned with *growth*. It will be examined against expected growth of sales, desired rate of return, acceptable cost of capital, consistency with present managerial capability, and so on. It will also be examined against estimates of conditions such as future consumer habits, changes in technology, trends in government regulation, and predicted actions of competitors.

In contrast, some proposals fall into a class concerned with *defensive actions*. These, for example, try to assure sources of supply or access to markets. Defensive proposals often integrate backward by acquiring suppliers or sources of raw materials or integrate forward by acquiring or establishing one's own distributors and retailers. In contrast to growth proposals, the evaluation of defensive proposals estimates the decrease in future sales and rates of return the firm would suffer if it did not integrate backward or forward. On the other hand, if the firm does integrate backward or forward primarily for defensive purposes, managers and planners must assess the risks of being saddled with high cost, underutilized assets.

Another class of proposals is concerned with maintaining *equity* in the firm's relations to different stakeholders such as employees, the local community, and so on. In contrast to growth and defensive proposals, one must assess how seriously a change in the pattern of equity may jeopardize present productivity as well as the firm's ability to attract competent personnel in the future. For example, in this class of proposals managers and planners may have to evaluate closing a marginally profitable, increasingly obsolete plant, absorbing some people and equipment at an existing plant, but disemploying the majority of the work force.

The review of balance requires that managers and planners take a holistic, integrated view. They have to step back from specific proposals which have different time spans, fall into essentially noncomparable classes, and which advance the interests of one division more than another, sometimes to the detriment of total corporate performance.

Components of balance

Managers should consider these questions: How good is the balance between long-term and short-term projects? Long-term investments with higher risk and stretched-out income streams are often the foundation that must be laid for the firm's future business. Short-term investments with more certain and quicker payoffs have limited life, but increase the risk that the firm will become more deeply committed to increasingly vulnerable markets and obsolete products.

How good is the balance among different classes of projects—growth, defense, and equity? Growth projects, for example, tend to increase the firm's vulnerability to problems of supply and distribution. So, there is a need to include a number of defense-anticipating projects even if they lower the estimated overall rate of return.

How good is the balance of investments among different divisions? When divisions are considered separate profit centers, they naturally tend to press their own interests with minimal regard for other divisions which, after all, are competitors for limited resources. Balancing starts with consideration of each division's estimated future financial performance. This criterion, however, has to be examined against the firm's overall strategy. For example, one may conclude, as General Motors did in 1933, that it would be best for the firm to alter division boundaries and policies and thereby open new opportunities to declining divisions. Instead of all growth being concentrated in one division, others are allowed to participate. The original growth division may or may not grow as rapidly as previously estimated, but the firm overall may be better off financially. Also, the firm retains several divisions of more manageable size instead of moving toward one giant division which becomes increasingly difficult to manage and control.

Then there is this question: If we successfully implement the accepted proposals, what kind of firm will we be? Is that the balance we intended?

Finding answers to these questions of balance requires managers and planners who make judgments from an integrated view of the firm's internal and external environment. They must conceptualize relationships among many noncomparable factors. For example, rate of return, vulnerability of the firm, distant opportunities, obligations to stockholders, and equity in using resources. Reviewing balance requires managers and planners who can go beyond straightforward extrapolations of existing data. The judgments to be made require policy makers who can visualize patterns in goals, actions, and consequences which are not evident to less astute observers.

A case of faulty balance

A poor review of balance leads to lopsided policies—policies which usually emphasize short-term, tangible gains with minimal change in present practices. Thus, faulty balance usually errs by giving inadequate attention to long-term, less tangible needs which require changes in present operations.

A classic illustration of a poor review of balance occurred in American Woolen Company. Following World War II, the company earned the highest profits in its history meeting pent-up civilian demand for woolens. At the same time, competitors were introducing new techniques for weaving wool. Sales of synthetic fibers—rayon, nylon, and dacron—and blends were small but growing in market share. American Woolen had more than ample earnings to increase its efficiency weaving woolens and develop the technology to become a leader in weaving synthetic fibers. Instead, it invested minimally in improving efficiency to weave woolens and disregarded the synthetics. From its pinnacle of earnings the company plummeted to bankruptcy in the 1950s.[13]

FACTORS AFFECTING A REVIEW

Several factors can increase stress in the organization and should be considered before initiation of a review of the policy process using the problem-solving model. These factors are the general manager's attitude, the pattern of division relations with the corporation, and the firm's recent financial and operating performance.

General manager's attitude

It is important to clarify several key points with the general manager regardless of whether his initial attitude toward reviewing the policy process is positive or negative. The general manager needs assurance that the review will not interfere with decisions already made and will not change the process in ways he cannot control. If the review is used by planners or other managers as an indirect method of pressuring the general manager to revise specific decisions, he is bound to be skeptical and to disapprove a review. Therefore, at the outset, the following ground rules should be defined.

First, past policy decisions will be examined only to determine and illustrate steps in the existing policy process. The examination will not revise any policy decisions. Only the general manager, if he wishes, may reopen a policy decision.

Second, the review may touch on some issues that aroused conflict in the past. These issues will be examined to the extent that they clarify the policy process. But, initially they will be stated in general, abstract terms if necessary. If they fan old conflicts into disruptive behavior, they will be temporarily set aside or replaced with other less conflictful illustrations of the policy process.

Third, the reviewers are not a decision-making group. They may only make recommendations to the general manager. In turn, he may approve, or disapprove with or without an explanation, or ask for additional information.

Fourth, the review will be conducted by a task force of managers and planners selected with the general manager's approval. He will help the team plan the review and will periodically hear and discuss their reports of progress. In addition, an outside consultant may be needed because of his knowledge of different concepts and approaches to the policy process, because of his ability to interview and gather data in delicate situations without having a vested interest in the outcomes, and because of his familiarity with the conditions needed to keep the review on track.

Next, we should obtain from the general manager his image of the present policy process. We should explore how his view is similar to and different from the problem-solving model (Figure 7-1) that will guide the review. The discussion introduces the general manager to the model and enables him to highlight activities which he believes could especially benefit from a review.

Finally, we should ask the general manager which policy decisions he does not want reopened, who he thinks might want to reopen them, and why; which policy decisions aroused strong conflict, who were the parties in the conflict, and how was it dealt with; and ideally, what changes would he want in the policy process.

The ground rules establish boundaries for the review. The discussion of the model acquaints the general manager with its content. Otherwise, his attitudes are principally affected by his desire not to be distracted from the press of immediate business problems or by a vague feeling that a review may increase tension in his management group without making a productive contribution. These concerns must be dealt with explicitly before a review can begin.

Division relations with the corporation

A division's relations with corporate managers and planners may be close and interdependent or distant and autonomous. In a close, interdependent relationship, the great influence of corporate managers in the division policy process makes their cooperation a necessity. A review of the policy process helps identify how the normal tension in corporate-division relations can be managed to contribute to the formulation of better policies. A task force composed of corporate and division people follows naturally from the prior close working relationship.

When a division's relations to the corporation are distant and autonomous, there are two levels of review. One takes place within the division which operates largely as a self-governing profit center. The second takes place at the corporate level where division product-market strategies are negotiable inputs to corporate financial and investment strategies.

In the case of distant, autonomous relations, division general managers and planners tend to interpret a corporate proposal to review the policy process as a potential encroachment on division autonomy. The division general manager therefore seeks assurance that the review is not a first step toward restricting his division's autonomy. Acceptance is highest if the division managers and planners initiate and conduct the review themselves. When the division planners do not have necessary skills, a second alternative is for them to consult corporate planners, but conduct the review themselves.

In a few instances corporate planners have pressed a review of a division's policy process because they disagreed with the division's strategy. In each instance the review was resisted and the division's relations with corporate planners were strained. If corporate management disagreed with the division's strategy, it should have raised the issue directly. Since they did not, the corporate planners' efforts to alter division strategy under the guise of a review of the policy process were seen as unsupported corporate staff interference which the division resented and quashed.

Recent performance

A general manager who is struggling to turn around a division or corporation that is unprofitable and rapidly nearing bankruptcy is not inclined to review the policy process, especially if his tenure is in jeopardy. His immediate concern is to cut all nonessential costs to get his organization back to an even keel. In such a situation there are two helpful steps. One is to ask the general manager to define a level of financial performance at which he believes it would be possible to consider a review proposal.

When does he believe that level might be reached? The second step is to accept the general manager's concern about short-term performance, then help to review the current definition of problems and opportunities and the alternatives generated to deal with them. Planners who can accept the general manager's short-term goals and show how to blend them into a long-term strategy develop credibility. On the other hand, during financial stress, planners who harp on long-term issues without relating them to constructive short-term actions are labeled blue-sky thinkers.

In some instances, when a new general manager has recently been appointed to take over a poorly performing division, the new manager is especially receptive to a review of the policy process. It enables him to get to know the division's planning process quickly. Also, a review encourages a balanced view of short-term needs and long-term goals and helps the firm quickly design an integrated plan.

Generally, however, it is best to review the policy process when a firm's recent performance has been good. Then, managers and planners can describe the process with minimal defensiveness and without feeling they are being diverted from urgent, short-term problems.

CONCLUSION

The problem-solving model described here is a comprehensive framework for reviewing and improving the policy process. It poses questions which diagnose how the policy process operates. It adds important information to the actor and procedure models. Each step in the problem-solving model, from scanning status to reviewing balance, is complex and merits careful study. The review is best done by a task force of managers and planners, aided by an outside consultant, and convened with the general manager's approval.

It is important to obtain the general manager's understanding and acceptance of the model and to have his participation in defining the scope and focus of the review. The general manager's attitudes depend on his belief that a review of the process will improve future policy formulation rather than reopen established policies or arouse disruptive conflict. Autonomous divisions are receptive to reviewing their policy process when corporate planners aid the division staff rather than use the project as an indirect attempt to change the division's current strategy.

It is difficult for a general manager to review the policy process when his organization is performing so poorly that it may not survive. It is helpful, though, to establish a level of performance at which a review would be feasible and then to assist the general manager in integrating short-term actions so they provide some potential for dealing with long-term problems and opportunities.

Generally, it is desirable to review the policy process comprehensively when the firm is doing well. Then, managers are more receptive and better able to use the results to exploit opportunities and avoid threats.

8. The Board of Directors

I t is increasingly evident that we have to think more carefully about managing the board of directors. Even though the board meets only once a month, it is a vital, functioning part of the organization. It must be managed effectively because it carries ultimate responsibility for directing and overseeing the organization. There is growing disenchantment with boards that contribute little more than legally required voting ceremonies.

EFFECTIVENESS AND POWER

The board has great power which critics claim it frequently does not use effectively. Many causes of ineffectiveness can be cited: overdependence on operating management, inadequate knowledge of the business, excessive desire to support incumbent management—to name a few. Some boards are unwilling to confront ineffective managers. Others are composed of directors with too little time and commitment to perform their duties properly.

Nevertheless, the board has the power to approve objectives and ratify policy. It has the power to review financial plans and performance, and to evaluate the competence of executives. The board's true power is so great that we cannot allow it to be used casually, incompetently, or irresponsibly.

All that we know about management must be applied to the board so that it becomes the best-managed part of the organization. This goal is not easily attained. Neither is it particularly attractive to strong, independent top executives who prefer a docile board.

MANAGERIAL ROLE VS. LEGAL LIABILITY

Much has been written about the duties of a director, the need for outside directors on every board, and the length of a director's term of office.[1] Board misfeasance and malfeasance have received special attention. For example: use of insider information, conflicts of interest in business dealings, and taking imprudent financial risks. Stockholder suits are increasingly common and few directors will serve without liability insurance.[2]

For the majority of directors these concerns diminish and constrain the board's managerial role. They stimulate decisions whose foremost goal is to avoid litigation.

Let us not dwell on what directors might do that subsequently may be imprudent or "illegal." That will continue to receive attention from regulatory agencies and jurists.[3] Rather let us concentrate on what the board might not be doing—its omissions of management.

We shall discuss several aspects of the board's work that offer opportunities for improvement. These are:

1. Managing the organization
2. Initiative in self-examination
3. Orientation and development
4. Succession policy
5. Relationships with management
6. How the board works as a group

MANAGING THE ORGANIZATION

The work of the board can be divided into two types of decisions: (1) decisions in which the major factors are known and can be predicted with a high degree of certainty, and (2) decisions in which the major factors are unknown or partially known and for which predictions are relatively uncertain.

Stewardship

The stewardship function of the board is composed mainly of decisions of the first type. In general, these are near-term decisions with a time horizon of 1 year or less, dealing with relatively well-structured situations. These include, for example, short-term goals for growth in sales, assets, and working capital. They also include approval of budgets for operating expenses, short-term manpower and borrowing policy, and reviews of recent financial results which may affect current decisions. There are usually well-developed procedures for these decisions. If there are not, there should be, because they are repetitive, and the factors are well known and predictable.

Directorship

The board makes its unique contribution to an organization by providing counsel for decisions of the second type—those dealing with situations with high uncertainty. This is the directorship function of the board. Such decisions are longer range, with a time horizon of more than 1 year usually and extending up to 5 years and sometimes to 10 years.

There is, however, a general principle of how managers use their time that applies here. Activities with well-developed solution procedures drive out activities for which there are not well-developed procedures. A routine analysis is familiar, gives an impression of control and a feeling of accomplishment. Non-routine situations, or so-called nonprogrammed activities, are unfamiliar, give an impression of disorganization, and often leave an unclear feeling of accomplishment. Dealing with nonroutine situations is demanding, time-consuming, and often frustrating, but this is where the board makes its major contribution.

Need for conditional planning

To fulfill its directorship function, the board must rely on conditional planning. In conditional planning we assume a possible condition will exist in the future and then explore how we might best prepare for it. This is useful, systematic, projective analysis. Conditional planning makes projections about the nature of the business, the nature of competition, and the nature of the market. It explores tentative decisions about policies, organization, and personnel needed to respond to, and possibly lead, these projections to best advantage.

Let us take an example from the finance industry. Suppose the board of a savings and loan association felt that in the future, say 5 years, the lending powers of associations will be broadened and low-cost electronic data processing equipment will be widely available. Suppose also that commercial banks will attempt to increase their share of time deposits and will increasingly enter mortgage financing. Advertising and promotion by competitors will increase substantially, and the number of college graduates interested in careers with financial organizations will rise. Each of these conditions would be projected in greater detail. Their effects on competition, on the market, and on the company would be studied and several courses of action would be devised.

Take the first instance of broadened lending powers. If they are broadened, what is most likely to be the form of the new lending powers? How large is the market? How does it differ from home financing? Who are the major institutions that have these lending powers now? What information can we get about examples of successful practices in these institutions? What will be the major elements of competition? What will it cost to make and service these loans? What personnel do we now have who know this field or who might be trained? What criteria should we use for deciding how far, if at all, we should enter this new market? If we do decide to go ahead, what should our organization look like?

Multiple Futures. In conditional planning we attempt to encircle the future since no one knows it exactly. We usually make three projections: a most likely projection, say with an estimated 50 percent chance of occurring; an optimistic projection with an estimated 25 percent chance of occurring; a pessimistic projection with an estimated 25 percent chance of occurring. Goals, policies, plans, and budgets are developed for each of the projections. As the future unfolds and converges with a particular projection, the board has the benefit of plans that have anticipated difficulties. It can choose from courses of action derived by rational analysis of a simulated future. It can avoid hasty, limited responses to surprise and emergency.

The timing of a future event is not critical in conditional planning. If the event occurs sooner than predicted, then appropriate plans are put into effect earlier. If it occurs later than predicted, then we delay administration of certain plans.

Reviewing the Spectrum. Top management's tendency is to concentrate the board's attention on the most likely projection since that is the plan it wants the board to approve. Although it may be unpleasant and time-consuming, the board must insist on discussing pessimistic or worst-case projections. It must ask for these projections and for managerial plans of response. The board must also ask for optimistic or best-case projections. Even these plans can have flaws. For example, when sales grow faster than the most likely projection, there may be deficiencies in capacity, finances, and human resources. Quality may deteriorate and the firm's future position in the market may be endangered.

The well-managed board understands the firm's intended plans, but it also prepares for the unintended, pessimistic case and the unexpected, optimistic case.

INITIATIVE IN SELF-EXAMINATION

The board's position at the top of the organization without any immediate, direct superior makes review and improvement of its work particularly difficult. Improvement of the board's work should not come from reluctant submission to outside forces. In the final analysis the board must rely on itself, on its own members—individually, in subgroups, and in total group—to review its own performance.

Self-examination is uncomfortable. Few of us like to analyze our poor decisions, oversights, or errors in judgment. Self-examination is delicate. Few of us can be told of errors without becoming defensive and disregarding the information. Hazardous as it may be, the hazards of the board ignoring self-examination are even greater.

It is an implicit responsibility of every board to seek actively its own improvement. No one can do this for the board. No one in the organization has the power to do it. Consultants and advisors can be helpful, but the members of the board know better than anyone how the board works and what needs improvement. The members of the board must take the initiative.

An individual member of the board can take the first step by proposing self-study and development as a formal activity for the board. Of course he must have the interest and support of other members. To start, members usually look at such issues as: What can be done to improve the preparation of directors for board meetings? How can we conduct meetings of the board so there is adequate, open discussion of the significant issues? How can we improve our planning process?

Orientation of new directors

Most boards consist of continuing members and new members. The continuing members have had several years of service with the board. They are familiar with its procedures, with some of the history of the organization, and with some of its unresolved problems. The new members do not have this background. They need it, however, to contribute effectively. Orientation of the new member should not be a haphazard process. A director's time and counsel are too valuable to waste on ferreting out information from chance experiences and discussions at board meetings. One approach is to have a continually updated set of briefing materials for new members. This includes information about the organization, its personnel, the board's procedures, the board's members, competition, recent decisions, minutes of several preceding meetings, existing policies, current problems, and other items members of the board believe will be helpful.

In addition, it is useful for at least one continuing member of the board to be paired with each new member. The continuing member would meet with the new member before board meetings and brief him on procedures, history, and so on, and on the meaning of the items on the agenda. This not only results in an informed director, it also helps new members feel that they are being welcomed into a council that has given serious thought to how to make best use of each person's time and skill.

Development of directors

The development of continuing members also deserves careful attention. The conditions under which a business operates and even the very nature of the business can change radically in a period of 5 years. New concepts, new methods, new technologies, and new legislation are introduced at such a rapid rate that continuing education and development of our adult population is a major national need. The college graduate finds his knowledge dated in 5 years and obsolete in 10 years. This is no less true for directors.

The continuing directors need guidance and help in charting the course of their own development. It is not enough to assume that directors know what has to be known or that they will acquire this knowledge on their own at their personal expense. Development at the level of the board proceeds best if a subcommittee, with the assistance of knowledgeable members of management, is designated to take on this responsibility. It requires continual assessment of the capabilities of members and how these might be improved to better serve the board.

Such a subcommittee would keep abreast of trends and new developments. It would decide on how to keep the board best informed. One of several directors could be asked to attend seminars or special outside conferences on a special subject and report to the board. Outside authorities familiar with new concepts or new technologies could be invited to seminars with the board. Members of management who are specialists in certain areas could be sent to specific programs and asked to report to the board. There is no shortage of methods. The important point is that the board needs an organ that systematically concerns itself with the board's development. That organ would plan and finance participation of directors in development activities.

SUCCESSION POLICY

Among its several responsibilities the board has the challenging task of planning its own composition and replacement. This is a task in which the board can show its true mettle. No group likes to think about change in its membership and few members look forward to separation from the group. Nevertheless, the board must rise to the challenge if it is to provide the organization with active, dedicated, forward-looking direction.

In upper and middle management it is customarily the responsibility of the manager to recruit and train his successor. Although the process is slightly different, this is no less true for the board. Succession policies should allow for the continual introduction of new competence and the infusion of new views within a stream of prudent management.

Importance of heterogeneity

In general, a group like the board makes better decisions than a single individual to the degree that members differ and use these differences to stimulate more comprehensive analysis than would be done by one person alone. When the members of a group are similar in background and in views, they tend to reinforce each other's biases and to concur in their blind spots. The best guiding principle for board succession policy is one that is also true for portfolio management—it is planned diversification.

A sound succession policy builds planned heterogeneity into the board. There should be heterogeneity in age, in length of service with the board and in knowledge and training. The rules that assure this diversity in the board are sometimes harsh in that occasionally a competent director is replaced because of what seems to be an arbitrary procedure. A good set of succession rules, however, is particularly needed by the board to assure that the replacement of less competent directors also occurs without splitting the board with personal antagonism and rancor.

Some elements of an effective succession program are as follows. Directors should systematically vary in background. Practice suggests directors with training in law, manufacturing, finance, marketing, science, public affairs, economics, and recently electronic data processing and real estate.

The retirement age for directors should be no more than 5 years beyond that for operating managers. Sometimes this will be severe but more often it will avoid misunderstanding and conflict. Directors should be about evenly divided among the three age brackets of less than 45, 45–60, and above 60 to prevent overloading the board with too many members who will retire at the same time. Diversity in age also provides diversity in outlook, initiative, and risk-taking.

These guides deal with several difficult issues in the succession process. Many boards prefer not to have such definitive statements. They argue that such principles seem arbitrary. They say that the long period of indoctrination makes low turnover among directors desirable. The lack of definitive statements, however, often results in a board with restricted vision and decreasing vitality. The argument that a director needs long service to learn the business loses meaning if there is a systematic program for developing new directors.

RELATIONSHIPS WITH MANAGEMENT

The relationship between the board and management should change as a business grows and as management's competence increases. The board should review this relationship periodically, otherwise practices will persist that should have been discontinued. Decisions will be retained that should have been delegated. For example, it is not unusual in small and medium businesses for directors to perform operating services. At one time these services might have helped an overburdened staff. An established organization, however, should have adequate staff to perform all operating work. Members of the board should not provide services and at the same time direct and evaluate management.

The policy vs. operations dilemma

The distribution of decision power between the board and management needs constant review. The principle that the board should limit itself to policy and leave operations to management is not easy to apply. Problems do not come with labels separating them into "policy" or "operations." Making this distinction can be a continual source of conflict between management and the board, when the real questions are: Who will decide what? Why?

Misunderstandings develop when the board appears to be overly involved in the details of operation, especially in the selection, assignment, and compensation of personnel. For example, when it is concerned about financial results, it may alter budget decisions, modify market development programs, and review pricing strategy. The board should clarify what boundaries it is setting and what discretion it is allowing. In transmitting its decisions, it should explain the reasons behind the boundaries and give examples of decisions within the discretion of management.

Improving the working relationship between the board and management requires the participation of both parties in a joint review and evaluation of current practices. Each should regularly consider two questions. The board should ask, "What can we do that would be helpful to the chief executive officer and other top managers? What can the chief executive, and other managers, do that would be helpful to us?"

Top management should ask similar questions, but from its view of the relationship. "What can we do that would be helpful to the board? What can the board do that would be helpful to us?" Serious consideration of these questions would in itself represent major progress in improving the relationship.

Answers to these questions are only the beginning of the improvement effort. Differences in the answers are informative. They reveal expectations that are not being met. The issue is not who is right and who is wrong. Rather, it is what are better ways to distribute planning and decision making between the board and management so that jointly they guide the organization more effectively.

Relations with middle management

Sometimes the board's relationships are limited to the chief executive officer. It is valuable for other top managers to know the board and to observe its deliberations. It is also useful for middle managers to hear discussions of issues and policies affecting their responsibilities. Many of the presentations to the board depend on reports by middle managers. Furthermore, the board's decisions ultimately will be implemented by these managers so communication between the two is invariably helpful.

The board and top management should plan the goals and methods for bringing the board and middle management in closer communication. It must be made clear, however, that contact between the board and middle management is not made because of reduced confidence in top management. Rather, it indicates that the board and top management have such mutual confidence that they cooperate to develop middle managers.

HOW THE BOARD WORKS AS A GROUP

As everyone knows, working in a group is quite different from working alone. Yet the literature treats directors as independent, isolated individuals. However, the board's effectiveness depends on each director's behavior, which in turn depends on what each director feels free to say when the board meets as a group and how others respond.

Contrasting views

For several reasons, boards resist reviewing how they work as a group. Directors usually have high social sensitivity, a strong sense of pride, and a desire not to embarass or publicly offend fellow directors. They are articulate and skilled at appearing agreeable in the most vexing circumstances. Also they generally believe that proper board meetings adhere to a prepared agenda, parliamentary procedure, and impersonal debate. And they know this format well. Directors therefore feel that their social skills and extensive experience make them adept at working in a group. Furthermore, directors feel it is below the board's station to open itself to such a review.

Yet, if directors observed middle or lower level groups of managers circumventing issues or discussing them as superficially as many boards do, they would demand immediate changes in management. The paradox is that a board would not tolerate lower management groups operating the way it often does.

Although it takes courage, skill, and agreement among board members to review their process, the methods for analyzing how a group works are well known and have been widely used in managerial groups.

Some opening questions

When studying the board as a group, we should consider several questions. For example: How do important issues get raised and discussed? Is the climate defensive, low in trust, and uncritical? How well do members listen? Do some members have more power than others? Is the board divided into rigid factions? Do directors feel it is hard to raise issues or to explore them adequately? Do some members dominate the board? Do directors feel forced to align with one or another faction? If so, the board can improve how it works as a group.

There are two common methods for dealing with problems of group operation. One is to wait for the chairman to act. The other is to block opponents by clever but legitimate use of parliamentary procedure. Both approaches leave much to be desired. Neither gets to root causes.

The first drops the problem in the chairman's lap expecting him alone to resolve the conflicts the members create. Often, the members are intransigent and unwilling to examine their role in the problem; they want the chairman to resolve it, by which they mean constrain their opponents.

Parliamentary blocking is a method of despair. Directors are saying it is too difficult to explore views constructively in search of a productive solution. When they use Roberts Rules to end search and impose a course of action, the problems of group operation keep recurring.

Reviewing the board's process

The board, like all other groups, has a process—a way of working. This should be distinguished from the customary notion of procedure. Procedure means have an agenda, have a discussion, follow Roberts Rules, and vote. In many meetings the agenda is limited to items acceptable only to the person who controls the agenda. Often this is the chief executive officer. The discussion is superficial and avoids controversial points. Voting is often ceremonial consent or is an instrument to suppress discussion or conflict. Such meetings follow a procedure, but their process—their way of working—is not very good.

An effective board manages itself by reviewing the way it works. The directors are aware that the group process can inhibit or facilitate planning and action. The board alone or with specialized help analyzes its difficulties and builds an atmosphere of nondefensiveness and increasing mutual trust. It experiments with defining and exploring issues. When the board faces conflict it does not place unrealistic demands on the chairman or retreat to Roberts Rules. The directors have enough skill and shared confidence so that all members try to clarify differences and create new solutions rather than withdraw or block each other.

CONCLUSION

The board, because of its power, can be a source of strength or a significant obstacle to an organization. The job of a director, if done properly, is demanding and difficult.[4]

The board must devote itself to examining projections of an uncertain future and evaluating the organization's proposed responses—a difficult, nonroutine activity. Directors must initiate systematic examination of the board's work. The board must take steps to orient new members and develop continuing members. The board should plan its own succession with devotion and diligence. The board has responsibility to build cooperative relationships with management and to foster managerial growth. Directors must develop awareness of how the board operates as a group and must build a climate conducive to effective problem solving.

The board must rely on projections of an unknown future to make decisions that affect an entire organization for years to come. Managing the board requires more than established procedures and parliamentary rules. The board is, after all, a living, changing group of human beings bearing enormous responsibility. It requires continual self-review and planned development.

PART 3
LIVING WITH KNOWLEDGE

9. Stability and Change

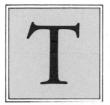

T he advent of knowledge constantly changes the boundary between what is stable and what is changing. The computer industry provides an awesome example of how knowledge drives the rapid, continuous interplay of stability and change. The first commercially available computers in the 1950s were gigantic brutes with miniscule, sluggish memory capabilities. An electromechanical technology for designing and producing memory devices such as rotating magnetic drums and mercury delay lines became a stable part of the industry. That stability lasted about 10 years, during which period the industry diligently worked behind the scenes on the next major change—the magnetic-core lattice memory.

The cycle of stability and change repeated with increasing frequency during the subsequent 15 years. Advances occurred in the use of tapes, disks, integrated circuits, monolithic circuits, virtual memory, and bubble memory. The industry became an outstanding example of how knowledge puts management on a roller coaster of stability and change.

TWO CRUCIAL DEMANDS

Management in a knowledge society faces two crucial demands—managing stability and managing change. Change in turn has a well-structured, short-term, operational component and an ill-structured, long-term, strategic component.

There is also in a developed knowledge society a pervasive undercurrent of uncertainty stemming from two major sources. One is internal uncertainty generated by management and consisting of poor decisions, unnecessary delays, and misallocation of materials. It also includes poor use of manpower, misuse of equipment, and failure to solve recurring problems. The other is external uncertainty—economic, political, and social—arising from forces beyond an organization's control or influence.

Management's first task is to reduce internal uncertainty by learning how to manage stability. Its second task is to cope with external uncertainty by developing strategies for change.

MANAGING STABILITY

By learning to manage stability, an organization reduces internal uncertainty and increases its efficiency. Yet managing stability is often considered unimportant, especially in organizations which extol creative improvisation and believe that stability can manage itself.

From experience, we know that 80 percent or more of what happens in an organization is repetitive. For example, making a deposit or withdrawal at a bank, placing a telephone call, or paying for a purchase in a department store. Repetitive tasks are invariably vital to large numbers of clients who depend on reliable performance. Management must reduce the ambiguity in such tasks so that performance need not be improvised or reinvented each day.

Also, a complex knowledge society spawns specialized organizations, such as U.S. Steel and General Motors, and specialized departments, such as sales and accounting, that increasingly depend on one another. Much of the instability in their relationship comes from the poor, uncoordinated performance of repetitive tasks—a condition that management can correct and control.

Managing stability is important regardless of whether an organization is small or large, in the private sector, or in the public sector. Small organizations, however, cannot afford staff with specialized knowledge to analyze the content of work, to assess systematically the performance of work, and to design motivating reward systems. Moreover, many large, government-related organizations are wary of tackling the management of stability because efforts to improve efficiency may decrease future appropriations, arouse worker resentment, and trigger adverse political reactions.

Guides for managing stability

Management can facilitate stability by introducing clarity of purpose, dependability in relationships, and predictability in behavior. Management must structure the organization to clarify jobs. It must assure that work is done on time and develop competent human resources. Following are several guides for managing stability.[1]

First, managers should take the lead in analyzing repetitive work. They should encourage probing questions: What repetitive work is being done? Who is doing it? When was it last studied? How can we improve its performance?

Second, managers should encourage the design of jobs which are intrinsically motivating. In a knowledge society, people prefer jobs which allow personal responsibility for meaningful work. These are jobs with task variety and some discretion in controlling the pace and sequence of work. After defining the repetitive content of a job, management should assure that it is acceptable to workers and beneficial to the organization.

Consider this simple experiment in the assignment of telephone repairmen. Each repairman was given responsibility for all telephone service in a selected part of a city, instead of working in a different area each day. Soon he knew all the clients in his area, and the special characteristics of their equipment. When something failed, the company and the clients knew he was responsible for repairing it. The repairman began doing preventive maintenance in his spare time. He took pride in his area and service improved because he was now anticipating breakdowns and working to minimize them.

Third, management should invest in training people to perform at a high level of proficiency. Society can provide a general education and basic skills. Thereafter, the organization must train workers to improve their competence in specific tasks.

Fourth, management should develop objective measures of performance and feedback systems that provide individuals with information they can use to plan and control their own behavior. Otherwise, the quest for improved efficiency is seen by workers as little more than an ambiguous, personal desire of the manager.

Finally, management should set high standards for the performance of repetitive work, reward achievement, and encourage pride in superior performance. If management considers repetitive work unimportant, so will the people who do it.

MANAGING CHANGE

The major challenges are in the second task of the manager's job—managing change, both operational and strategic.

Operational change

Operational change is short or medium term, with a 1- to 3-year horizon. It focuses on methods and procedures, personnel assignments, and use of materials. Operational changes are often needed to cope with the problems that come with stability. Inefficiency—the duplication of some activities and the omission of others—is a major problem of stability.

Duplication. Consider, for example, the duplication subscribers go through each time they file a medical insurance claim. Each claim requires filling out a handwritten form asking for basic information. In contrast, a person with an American Express credit card can travel around the world with less paperwork. The plastic card with his name and account number readable by a computer avoids duplication and reduces errors.

Insensitivity. Operational changes are also needed to correct organizational insensitivity. When organizations systematize repetitive work, they generally place their own needs above those of their clients. They select working hours and design forms and procedures for their own ease. These often are inconvenient and costly to clients. For example, most banks close in the early afternoon. In most cities only minimal medical services are available on weekends.

Covert Rewards. Operational changes are needed to counteract the covert reward of dysfunctional behavior that often comes with stability. Government agencies often provide the best examples. There are two kinds of errors a public servant may commit. One is to deny a citizen a service to which he is entitled. The second is to grant a citizen a service he may not be entitled to. The first error—denying the service—costs the public servant little or nothing; it simply returns the problem to the citizen who must forego the service or find some other means to get it. But, granting a person a service he may not be entitled to can be costly. It can lead to public embarrassment, severe reprimand, and difficulty in getting promoted.

Generally, there is little risk-taking in public bureaucracies because the reward system is unbalanced. It is safer for a public servant to say no or to tell a claimant to take his request elsewhere.

To offset this bias, management must systematically record and regularly review claims that have been denied. Only this way will it find clues to needed operational changes. Then it must train a cadre of individuals who can recognize when normal procedures are unsuitable and who can resolve such problems rather than pass them on to someone else.

The Vanishing Refund. Consider the following case illustrating how an organization can systematically deny legitimate claims without the knowledge of higher management. For many years auto supply stores and gasoline stations sold several brands of automobile batteries. In this case, a customer returned to a gasoline station a defective battery that had failed with 12 months remaining in the original 24-month warranty period. He asked for a pro-rata refund toward the purchase of a new battery. The station manager refused even though his station had sold the battery to the customer.

The customer called several people in the manufacturer's local sales division. Each person told him that only the station manager could give him a refund or else shifted the call to someone else. The indignant customer persisted and finally reached the national sales manager. The customer then handed the telephone to the station manager and told him to explain why he refused to grant the pro-rata refund. The station manager told the national sales manager that he had been unable to get reimbursement from the manufacturer for pro-rata refunds even though he had complained to the local sales office. So, for the last year he had stopped giving pro-rata refunds. If not for this persistent, angry customer the national sales manager would not have heard of the problem. Subsequent investigation showed it was widespread.

Middle Managers. Operational changes may be needed when middle managers become a barrier to an organization's growth. Especially prone to this are departments that must grow in response to new demands after lying dormant for several years. In banks these have often been the "back office" operations departments that process transactions.

Some middle managers attempt to augment their power by controlling minor decisions in spite of a growing workload. They may communicate selectively by withholding important information from their subordinates or their managers. As the organization grows, the functions of middle managers often must be changed to free them from the mentality of the small organization. They need help in learning to delegate and to act as competent intermediaries between higher managers and workers who become increasingly distant with growth.

STRATEGIC CHANGE

Strategic change is long term, usually 3 to 10 years. It focuses on values, goals, policies, organizational structure, and investments of capital and other resources. For example, IBM's evolution from a product line based on punched cards to a product line based on electronic computers. Or the automobile industry's move from large, high-horsepower cars to small, low-horsepower cars. Strategic situations are ill structured and have a number of important properties that affect the mode of organization the manager should use.

Understanding ill structure

Information. Strategic situations tend to be ill-structured because of incomplete, uncertain information about the distant future and dependence on the intentions and behavior of other organizations not under one's control. Most organizations face a highly uncertain external economic, political, and regulatory environment complicated by great dependence on other organizations and societies. For example, when IBM invested $6 million to build its first computer, there was little understanding of who would use it or how it would be used. Initial estimates forecast a total market demand of 15 to 20 computers. Also, competitors already had significant experience in product design and manufacturing.

Multinational firms face growing uncertainties in U.S. relations with the Soviet Union, European countries, Latin America, and Africa. These relations can be volatile and difficult to predict. U.S. dependence on oil-exporting countries amplifies the uncertainty of information.

Multiple Goals. Strategic situations involve multiple goals that are interrelated. Such situations are ill structured because the pursuit of one goal requires complex, nonlinear trade-offs with other goals. For example, in the farm equipment industry, International Harvester had to make complex trade-offs among product changes, plant modernization, market promotion and strengthening its distribution system in its competition with John Deere Company and others. At the national level, increasing Social Security benefits and providing a more comprehensive national health system mean that trade-offs must be made in economic development, military self-sufficiency, and agricultural development.

Causality. In an ill-structured situation, we do not know what causes what. There is interaction among multiple causes and effects, some inhibiting and some amplifying others' impact. For example, in a competitive market or in political negotiations, it is hard to know the causes and effects of actions by other crucial parties. Consider the unexpected decision of Egyptian President Sadat to visit Israel in 1977, the deposing of the Shah of Iran in 1979, and the Soviet move into Afghanistan. These events were unforeseen, as were their full outcomes.

Many Feasible Solutions. An ill-structured situation has almost an infinite number of feasible solutions. By closely following management's discussion, one can observe the emergence of a large set of feasible solutions. For example, in a planning meeting in a consumer goods company one manager proposed increasing the price of a product 10 percent, decreasing the market share, and investing $1 million in facilities to produce a *new* product. Shortly thereafter, a different manager proposed the exact opposite: decrease the price 10 percent, increase market share, and invest $1 million to expand facilities to produce the *existing* product. Each alternative and its opposite, as well as many proposals between and outside the range of these two, were feasible solutions.

Moreover, in the ill-structured situation, there often are no universally accepted, definitive criteria for choosing the best alternative from the large number of contradictory possibilities. In the example mentioned above, both managers argued with supporting data that their alternative provided superior return on investment. Each argued that his proposal was less risky: the investment in the new product because the existing product was becoming obsolete; the investment in the existing product because minor changes would extend its market life, whereas demand for the new product was based on controversial marketing tests.

Interpreting Results. Feedback about consequences usually occurs long after action—sometimes years later—in an ill-structured situation. Because of the long time lag and the complexity of causes, it is difficult and often misleading to attribute the consequences exclusively to one's actions. Golda Meir, a former prime minister of Israel, gave a humorous example of drawing simple cause-and-effect conclusions long after a decision. She said, "Moses was not such a great leader after all. If he had turned right instead left, then Israel would have had the oil today."

Self-Proclaimed Experts. Finally, an ill-structured situation is harrowing and bizarre because it is difficult to identify the expert advice-giver beforehand. However, there is no shortage of self-proclaimed experts; every specialist or administrator can claim to be an expert, and usually does. This dilemma is built into the ill-structured situation. With information uncertainty each can argue forcefully, but never with irrefutable proof, that he knows the future better than others. With causal uncertainty, each can argue that he knows the consequences of an action better than others. With goal complexity, each can assert that his proposed goals are more valid for the organization than others' goals. With many alternatives and no settled criteria for choosing among them, each can argue that his solution is rationally superior to others. Finally, with distant, inconclusive feedback, there is no way to prove what is right or wrong at the time we are making a decision. Consider the following classic case.

In the 1960s, when the United States government was considering subsidizing the development and construction of supersonic, commercial aircraft, there was heated argument for and against the proposition. Ultimately, billions of dollars and thousands of potential jobs were at stake. Specialists, advisors and representatives of aircraft manufacturers, the air transport industry, and passenger groups held forth with self-proclaimed expertise. Proponents argued that the plane was economically feasible, and if we did not build it the United States would lose its preeminance as the world's leading manufacturer of aircraft. Opponents argued with equal force and conviction that costs would be much higher than projected, passenger traffic would be much lower than predicted, and failure to build a supersonic transport (SST) would not adversely affect our world position.

France and England formed a consortium and built an SST, the United States decided not to. Almost 15 years after the decision and billions of dollars later we learned that the United States was right and France and England wrong. The SST could be cited as a symbol of national pride, but high operating costs, low passenger traffic, and insufficient sales of additional SSTs made it a financial disaster.

Avoiding Catastophe. Since strategic situations involve tremendous costs and high penalties for errors, it is crucial to find solutions which minimize the maximum loss and limit the downside risk. A decision process is needed that will avoid the catastrophic solution. In business, strategic decision making can be called "You Bet Your Company"; in international affairs, it can be called "You Bet Your Country."

Strategic problems clearly are ill-structured situations. There are effective and ineffective methods for dealing with strategic situations. The challenge to managers is to understand the difference and to develop skills in using the most effective methods.

DECISION MODES

There are two basic modes for dealing with strategic problems: a directive mode and a consultative mode.

Directive mode

In the directive mode the manager consults few people. He gets information from below, analyzes it himself, and draws his own conclusions. Occasionally he locates an expert and implements the expert's recommendation.

The directive mode relies on one individual. In an ill-structured situation, when the manager has the gifts of prophecy and wisdom, his solutions can be spectacularly effective. But relying on one individual also carries a high probability of selecting a catastrophic solution. Grasping the consequences of many alternatives in an ill-structured situation is often beyond one person's ability, especially when he is responding under stress.

It is therefore hazardous to use the directive mode for ill-structured situations. The manager may transfer goals and assumptions from a prior, well-structured situation to the current ill-structured situation where they are not relevant. Without the safeguards of exposure to questioning and consultation, he may treat a unique, distinct situation as if it were an old problem. He may resurrect old solutions he is familiar with instead of new concepts and creative improvisation.

For example, Dr. Edwin Land was the energizing force and creative genius behind the Polaroid Company's highly successful move into self-developing film for still photography. His decision to apply the same principles to a line of motion picture photography products in the late 1970s, however, proved to be a costly failure.

Ill-structured problems require the consultation of many people. They require a climate which permits asking probing questions. Assumptions, goals, costs, and consequences must be put under the light of searching inquiry. In the ill-structured situation, specialists may be available; but once their information and views have been shared, it is misleading to assume that any one of them is more or less expert than the other in choosing a good solution. Indeed, specialization often biases their choices. It is fruitless, therefore, to search for the single individual with the best solution; he cannot be identified. Rather, the manager must encourage probing questions and wide consultation so he can generate suitable goals, relevant criteria, and feasible alternatives.

Consultative mode

Organizations need a norm permitting questioning the decisions of higher authorities. Such a norm means that in problem discussions, managers, in business or government, can quickly move into probing each other's goals, assumptions, and alternatives without feeling that the conflict will destroy their organization. Contention is necessary to detect the pitfalls and low-quality strategies that should be avoided.

For example, the IBM management system is noted for its constructive use of contention at every level of the organization. Sales people are brought together regularly to review differences in approaches to prospects and clients. Operating groups and staff groups, after discussions among themselves to determine and enlarge the extent of their concurrence, frequently make separate presentations to higher executives and managment committees. Their agreements as well as differences are closely questioned. Ultimately a decision is made, but unresolved differences in proposals and evaluations are recorded.

Later, sometimes years later, when the results are finally in, the recorded differences are reviewed, and the superiority or deficiencies in the quality of data, logic, and judgments at the time the decision was made are factored into the reward system. The process encourages, systematizes, and rewards the use of consultation, contention, and concurrence.

Authorities. It is fitting that we admire authorities and experts and treat them with respect and dignity. But in ill-structured situations it is dangerous to hold self-proclaimed authorities or experts in such awe that they cannot be questioned. A person's wisdom must be proved in each new ill-structured situation. High position should not significantly shield managers from confrontation and questioning. The purpose is to avoid strategic catastrophe, a penalty none of us can afford. The purpose is not to embarrass or harass managers, although that unfortunately may be a by-product of a disorderly, emotion-laden questioning process.

In government, a parliamentary system builds questioning and probing into the core of a nation's strategic decision system. A prime minister often cannot form a cabinet without members of parties whose views differ from his. To act on a major strategic issue, the prime minister must have the consensus of his cabinet. Thus the decision system is open to the expression of differences. This does not make it an easy system to work in, but when the survival of a country, or an organization, is in the balance, managers may have to forego some emotional comfort to increase the probability that they will make effective strategic decisions.

When Harmony Hurts. Managers in business and government in the United States appear to be insulating themselves from views that differ from their own. Harmony and amiability are so highly valued that many organizations operate with ineffectual policies because managers are reluctant to risk unpleasantness by speaking up.

There has developed a substantial vested interest in past solutions. Although the United States has been a leading knowledge society, stimulating contention, imagination, and creative improvisation has become an increasingly serious problem in large organizations and in government agencies.

Misuse of Consultation. Managers should be aware that it can be detrimental to use the consultative mode to deal with well-structured situations. Managers often try to give others the feeling that they are participating in the decision process. When a manager involves people in a problem for which he has adequate information and clear criteria for making an acceptable decision, he is engaging in pseudoconsultation. When he involves others in lengthy discussions of trivial problems, he is engaging in pseudoparticipation. Most people recognize these ceremonies as a waste of time.

POWER AND KNOWLEDGE

Top management deals primarily with ill-structured problems. Hence, knowledge and its analysis are vital commodities at the top of an organization. When in high office, executives are keenly aware of the value of knowledge, critically analyzed and properly interpreted. Working with one's hands and feet at the top of an organization is neither feasible nor appropriate.

Power, however, is not the same as knowledge, and attaining high position does not anoint an individual with superior foresight or with exceptional insight into causes and consequences. Higher managers have wider access to information, but this is not knowledge of the future or of the responses of others.

When a higher manager has power but lacks knowledge, he can endanger his organization. Therefore, a higher manager must regularly update his knowledge so that he can question the assumptions of his advisors. He must search beyond the obviously favorable consequences of their recommendations to the wider, long-range effects. Thus the manager must continually reeducate himself, regardless of his power, so he can understand and evaluate the concepts his advisors use.

Top managers are usually willing to support education of middle managers. On the other hand, they often appear less willing to open themselves to new knowledge, especially when they believe they have found satisfactory solutions to current problems. They become adept at managing the current stability, but unless they reach out and stretch themselves with new knowledge, their management of change falters.

10. Industrial Citizenship

nowledge and industrialization march forward together, each supporting and stimulating the other. The combination inexorably changes society and alters fundamental aspects of our life such as family relations, the nature of work, and the path of adult development.

For example, knowledge of mining and smelting led to the iron and steel industry. This in turn led to advances in machine tools, production machinery, railroad transportation, and new knowledge in metallurgy. The spiraling development of knowledge and industry—repeated with internal combustion engines and automobiles; powered air flight; and electronics, telecommunications, and computers—pervasively affects us as individuals by modifying our relationships to each other, our organizations, and our society. What does being a competent citizen mean in such a society?

COEXISTING WITH ORGANIZATIONS

A competent industrial citizen contributes to the goals of his organization but also shapes and responsibly criticizes how organizations function in society. Citizenship, in this fundamental sense, is essential to dealing with a central problem of industrial democracy: maintaining the delicate balance of power between organizations and individuals.

Effective citizenship requires that we be inside and yet outside our organization. Inside the organization, we must define and attain worthwhile goals. Outside the organization we must be alert to dangerous imbalances of power. We must sense threats that, at one extreme, might subjugate the individual or, at the other, destroy the organization. And we must act to offset them. If we do not maintain the behavioral competence an industrial society requires, life will swing between chaotic turmoil and organizational tyranny.

This concept of industrial citizenship may seem too ambitious—a prescription beyond our attainment. One suspects, however, that this concept, so articulately expressed by Peter Drucker, is prophetic.[1] Only by understanding and learning to cope with the organizations we contrive can we survive and benefit from industrialization.

THE SHOCK OF INDUSTRIALIZATION

Cultural rifts are insidious; their deep, enduring effects on behavior are not readily apparent. Industrialization was not simply a change in technology, it was a revolutionary change in man's social condition that disrupted his relation to himself and his family. It changed his relation to his work and his fellow men and drastically altered his concepts of the meaning of life. These are human dilemmas of enormous proportions.

As industrial citizens we are on our own in our struggle to cope with these dilemmas.

The family in retreat

Industrialization persists in impairing the family; understanding this is fundamental to understanding an industrialized society.[2] In the preindustrial era, the family was the basic social unit and the basic work group. In this arrangement each person, from the youngest child to the oldest adult, was productive. The production group and the family were one and the same. Productivity, human relations, and conditions for the growth of children coincided.

Each person contributed to the needs of the family at the level of his capacity. Each person knew what he produced. Output was an extension of the person: it was the house he built, the tools and pottery he fashioned, the clothing he made.

Prestige accrued to the individual craftsman because quality was associated with his name. A man's work was his claim to status.

Industrialization changed these conditions and irrevocably altered man's behavior. In one vast sweep the rhythm and meaning of life changed. The family was disrupted. Man's independence, growth, and sense of competence were challenged.

In this process of social erosion, the industrial organization displaced the family. Men, women and children left each other early in the morning and returned home late at night. The family was fragmented, and its existence was threatened. The personal growth and integrity that children develop from patient, low-stress contact with adults was endangered. This is not to say that the family in preindustrial society was completely free of stress and poverty; however, in industrial society stress and poverty continue. Although they now take different forms and there are extensive social support and welfare systems, we cannot say that the afflictions of stress and poverty are less severe or debilitating than in the past.

Urbanization, conveniences, and the hollow family

By the middle of the twentieth century, although many assumed that the family had accommodated to industrialization, it was to suffer additional injury. The suburb—the middle-class commuter's bedroom community—became the modern, picture-window version of the fatherless family. The generation gap that followed was not the result of a difference in age, it was the harvest of an age of indifference. Industrialization spawned urbanization and together they continued to trap the family.

Many of the children of the past three decades, now the teenagers and young adults of today, saw their parents as strangers, which indeed they were. Start with the 8-hour workday, add 2 or more hours for travel, lunch, overtime, trips out of town, weekend work, and for many moonlighting on a second job, and the middle-class parent was away from home 12 or more hours a day often 6 or 7 days a week. Not much of a change from 100 years ago, even though the legal workday had been shortened.

Industrial conveniences, such as automobiles and television, raised the standard of material living but also introduced new opportunities for family separation. Automobiles allowed instant mobility and shopping trips often substituted for serious examination of child-parent relations. Television competed with parents as a model, and watching television encouraged emotional isolation in the presence of others. Members of a family could now avoid each other at home as well as at work.

The hip and beat generations' turn to drugs and to mass movements were, in part, responses to the hollow family. The deprivation of meaningful contact with reliable parents during crucial periods of growth had to be filled. There was a search for relatedness and serenity, the qualities that a hollow, industrialized family failed to provide.

Forbidding the employment of children in industry "does not solve the problem of the child in industrial society. The family is still as necessary as ever as a biological and especially as an emotional unit. . . . Disturbances of the emotional bond which in traditional societies are not much more than minor nuisances become severe crises and the cause of maladjustments, 'neuroses' or 'complexes', destructive alike of individual and of family life."[3]

FUTURE INDUSTRIAL CITIZENS

If we are to understand citizenship in our society, we must deal with industrialization's disruption of the relationship between children and their parents. The distance between children and parents is evident at an early age; most children are confused when asked about their father's work. They see him leave home early and return late, often tired and irritable, so they conclude that work must be unpleasant. Behavioral scientists call this socialization—the process by which a person learns the values and the required behavior of his society.

For many young people, organizations seem to exact such severe human costs that society may unwittingly be teaching them that the price is too high for the resulting material benefits. Many are not convinced that economic growth necessarily improves social well-being. They often are skeptical after reviewing family life, poverty, and unemployment in the nation. An industrial society that ignores the uneasiness and doubts of its young citizens imperils its future.

Many individuals have expressed concern about the alienation from self, from family, and from work that seems inevitable with industrialization. As we move toward postindustrial society, the competent industrial citizen petitions management to shape organizations and work so they support individual growth, integrity, and mutual concern.

THE IMPACT OF ORGANIZATIONS

Dependence

Industrialization increased man's vulnerability. It shifted productivity to the organization and made individuals interchangeable and dispensable. The organization combines the work of many people to make a useful product, whether it is a pencil or an automobile. Individuals depend on access to an organization.

Without access they become economically destitute, psychologically depressed, and ultimately social outcasts.[4]

Even while working in an organization man is still psychologically vulnerable and socially anonymous. It is often difficult, if not impossible, to identify his work in the final product. It is one input lost among many. If he is a manager, his work is intangible and rapidly dissolves in a combination of ideas and efforts.

Prestige, man's public competence, depends more on his position in an organization than his work. People introduce and defer to each other by title, such as vice president, department manager, and so on, often knowing little about the real content or quality of each other's work. Thus, with increasing frequency it is less what a man does and more his title that has become the basis for status.

Adult development

The most important and most overlooked impact of an organization is how it aids or obstructs our development as adults. Mass production is more than a principle of technology, it is "a general principle for organizing people."[5] And it is not confined to manufacturing, but applies to all work—clerical, scientific, managerial, and so on.

Division of labor and specialization—the essence of industrial organization—has made many jobs repetitive and unchallenging and has discouraged human growth. Organizations may train a person for a particular job, but once this is accomplished, additional learning not obviously related to the job is often discouraged. Non-job-related learning is considered an uneconomical distraction. It provides no obvious benefit to the organization and may disrupt production.

There is a fundamental, continuing conflict between the organization's demands and the nature of man. Anthropologists tell us that man has the largest brain of all creatures, except the whale. Man can symbolize, think of past, present, and future, and imagine actions and consequences. Man survives and spreads his civilization principally because he is a problem-solving creature. His physical endowments are unimpressive.

Industrialization, however, organizes men to perform at a primitive level. Mass output is based on low-level physical and mental work. *Its most insidious effect, however, is to discourage personal growth not immediately related to one's job.*

The primary argument favoring the view that an organization must focus only on what a person contributes to the job to be done is that the enterprise must first and foremost meet its economic responsibilities. Emphasizing the economic purpose of the enterprise is understandable. But we cannot continue to overlook an organization's squandering of human resources when it ignores, restrains, or obstructs the development of its people.

Comparing management of human resources and other resources

We can analyze the organization's management of adult human resources by comparing it to the management of other resources. *The human potential to grow is like a public resource such as air and water. Whether or not it is needed to do a job, human beings come with it.*

Generally, economic measurements should guide a firm's decisions. Many management decisions, however, have been converted to legislative or moral decisions when economic measurements were incomplete or misguided. For example, the pollution of air and the contamination of water historically have been treated as moral issues. They got little attention because of incomplete, narrowly focused concepts of economics. Measurement of a firm's performance said the organization incurs no costs when it uses a public (free) good such as air or water.

The industrial citizen is faced with a dilemma: No single organization need account for its use of a public good, but the aggregate of all organizational use deteriorates the public environment.

In a competitive market it is unlikely that a profit-optimizing organization will hold itself morally accountable for an activity that has no cost in its profit and loss statement. Each organization uses traditional, limited economic measurements. Each will seek to minimize its costs, arguing it must do so to remain competitive. Ultimately the accumulated deterioration is bound to reach catastrophic levels.

Belatedly we discovered that in many cities people could no longer breathe the smog. They could no longer swim in lakes or drink water from their wells. Driven by a lack of organizational accountability but consistent with the firm's circumscribed economic goals, deterioration of public resources diminishes the "quality of life." It also ignores the elementary economics of aggregate national wealth. What was once an abundant, widely available, public good becomes a scarce, restricted, costly commodity.

SPOILAGE, DEPLETION, AND RECOVERY

Spoilage

The industrial citizen, whether manager, worker, or customer, is painfully learning that in every economic enterprise there is an ignored cost. It is not the cost of spoiling a public resource, because in the accounting system of the individual firm this costs nothing. It is the cost of returning spoiled resources to their original condition. It is a "recovery" cost which in our system of enterprise traditionally is not borne by the user organization. It is aggregated and called a public cost, one that everyone pays through taxation.

Depletion

We should clarify some subtle but crucial points about the language of spoilage. A public resource no longer usable by industry is depleted, not spoiled. Then the organization incurs a cost when it searches for replacement or substitute resources. Industry, however, can often use low-quality resources of air or water before they are depleted.

A resource still usable by industry but no longer usable by human beings, however, is spoiled. For example, a paper mill or a chemical plant can continue to discharge effluents into a lake long after it is unusable by people.

Spoilage/recovery

We shall describe four important properties of the spoilage/recovery process that help us understand the impact of organizations on individuals.

Deprivation. First, there is deprivation of resource use. When a resource is spoiled, we the industrial citizens who are collateral, nonindustrial users, are deprived of its use. A lake or river perfectly usable for industrial purposes may be unusable by local residents for the better part of their lifetime. For example, it has been estimated that it would take 20 to 50 years for Lake Erie to return to its original condition after all industrial pollution is stopped.

Costs. Second, costs are shifted from the organization to the industrial citizen. The organization still has a usable resource, but the individual who wants clear water must dig a deeper well or travel greater distances. He must invest in recovery facilities and pay for government regulatory agencies. Paradoxically, the victim of spoilage pays the costs of accommodation.

Prevention. Third, the costs of recovery usually exceed the costs of prevention. It is less costly to prevent contamination of water at the source than to remove the contaminating agents after pollution.

Recovery. Fourth, sometimes recovery may not be possible. Methods may not exist to reverse spoilage of physical resources and human resources. For example, experience in trying to rehabilitate human beings who have suffered psychological and social impairment indicates that reversibility is costly and difficult and frequently impossible. Drug addiction, alcoholism, psychosis, and many forms of neurosis may not be reversible. Historically, the recovery rate has been less than 20 percent of those treated.

Is human growth recoverable?

Now let us apply these concepts of spoilage/recovery to adult development and the organization's use of its human resources. Because of inadequate economic measurements, organizations will continue to feel little accountability for people. Organizations will continue to make primitive, low-quality demands of individuals. Human competence will be able to decay substantially before it is unusable by the organization.

That the organization will use few of a person's higher capabilities and may discourage growth are problems shifted to the individual. He will have to figure out how to recover and he will have to pay the costs. The spoilage/recovery process transfers these dilemmas to us, the industrial citizens. From the organization's view we are collateral users of ourselves.

If an organization spoils human beings by using them at a primitive level and discouraging their growth—how useful are these human beings to themselves?

The costs of recuperating from continued, low-level use of our human abilities are varied and not clear. Some individuals collapse into lethargy and disinterest. After work they must rest to rebuild their energy. It is hoped that they may one day consider growth activities. Others find untapped energy. Freed of organizational constraints they engage in frenzied, exhausting physical activities.

How well do individuals recover energy for growth and development? Prolonged indifference or discouragement of adult development by an organization inevitably leads most people to give up personal growth. Once confidence in the value of personal growth is lost, it is difficult to recover. For many people it is not recoverable.

Management's attitude
toward personal growth

Organizations of course must strive to increase productivity, but at the same time a positive attitude toward individual growth is critical.[6] People can be productive using few of their abilities. They can perform well-defined tasks and they can tolerate substantial monotony and repetition. But the organization's attitude toward their growth determines the meaning of their productivity. If management's attitude is negative, people feel exploited and become cynical.

The view that supporting human growth may interfere with productivity puzzles the industrial citizen. He cannot understand organizations that "turn man's capacity to grow into a threat to himself and his fellow man."[7]

Our quality of life occurs largely in our work organizations. There, if we are fortunate, we find opportunities for personal growth and for influencing our future. Few organizations, however, recognize that they are using human beings in ways that diminish man's ability to know and develop himself. When managers understand that human resources can be spoiled and wasted like physical resources, and when they can account for that spoilage in their economic measurements, then organizations will manage adult development—their free resource—more effectively.

MOTIVATION

Motivation is a paradox in industrial society. Theoretically, organizations strive to increase the output of individuals but in practice, many organizations demotivate people. Misapplication of our heritage of scientific management continues to plague us.

It is false logic to believe that because we study work by examining its constituent parts that we must therefore divide work into elementary tasks and assign each to an individual worker who repetitively performs the same activity.[8] Such an approach to job design concentrates on analysis and ignores integration. Such logic ignores the fact that man's specific contribution is always to perform many motions, to integrate, to balance, to control, to measure, to judge.[9]

Misunderstanding of scientific management has also encouraged the divorce of planning from doing. That planning is different from doing and contributes to easier, more effective work is a valuable insight. But the analytical distinction between planning and doing does not require that the planner and the doer be two different people.

These overextensions of scientific management arouse worker resistance to changes intended to improve productivity and stifle rather than develop the individual. The desire to maximize output has often led to routine, simplified work, and subordinates who are poorly informed, reluctant to dissent, and hesitant to be creative. Even under these conditions people can be productive, but in spite of rather than because of the organizational setting.

To get out of this motivation trap we need "to replace the externally imposed spur of fear with an internal self-motivation for performance. Responsibility is the only thing that will serve" and whether or not man wants it, the organization must demand it of him.[10]

To reach the goal of the responsible contributor, organizations should: (1) set high standards of performance; (2) provide the worker with the information needed to control himself; (3) provide opportunities for participation in decisions that affect work; (4) design jobs that consist of an integrated whole, embody some challenge, some element of skill or judgment; (5) include some planning in each job; (5) place individuals carefully and, if needed, modify jobs to match individual skills and interests.

Research repeatedly supports these suggestions, which humanize work and stimulate self-direction.[11] They encourage growth, self-correction, and the attainment of economic goals. But the problems of implementing these suggestions will continue long into the future.

The toll of low motivation is substantial and both the organization and we, as individuals, suffer. But as industrial citizens, we must take steps to make the organization motivationally attractive.

Modern organization makes demands on the individual to learn something he has never been able to do before: to use organization intelligently, purposefully, deliberately, responsibly. If he runs away from this task and its decisions, organization will indeed become the master. . . . To make our society free will require that the individual learn how to manage organization—how to make organization and his job in it serve his ends, his values, his desire to achieve.[12]

Thus, industrial citizenship is learning how to act in and on organizations to improve the quality of *our* life. We have great freedom to shape organizations. We must learn to use that freedom creatively and wisely. That is the unending challenge of industrial citizenship.

Notes

CHAPTER 1

1. W. J. J. Gordon, *Synectics,* Collier Macmillan, New York, 1968.

CHAPTER 3

1. See M. Deutsch, "Cooperation and Trust: Some Theoretical Notes," in R. Jones, ed., *Nebraska Symposium on Motivation,* University of Nebraska Press, Lincoln, Nebraska, 1962, pp. 275–319.

2. For a summary of some of the extensive research see C. R. Rogers, *On Becoming a Person,* Houghton Mifflin, Boston, 1961, pp. 39–58.

3. See J. R. Gibb, "Defense Level and Influence Potential in Small Groups," in L. Petrillo and B. M. Bass, eds., *Leadership and Interpersonal Behavior,* Holt Rinehart Winston, New York, 1961, pp. 66–81; M. B. Parloff and J. H. Handlon, "The Influence of Criticalness on Creative Problem Solving Dyads," *Psychiatry,* 1966, vol. 29, pp. 17ff.

4. J. R. Gibb, "Climate for Trust Formation," in L. P. Bradford, J. R. Gibb, and K. D. Benne, eds., *T-Group Theory and Laboratory Method,* Wiley, New York, 1964, pp. 279–301.

5. This situation is a variation of one presented in R. F. Maier, A. R. Solem, and A. A. Maier, *Supervisory and Executive Development,* Wiley, New York, 1959, pp. 308–315.

CHAPTER 4

1. W. G. Bennis, *Changing Organizations,* McGraw-Hill, New York, 1966. R. Likert, *The Human Organization,* McGraw-Hill, New York, 1967. D. McGregor, *The Human Side of Enterprise,* McGraw-Hill, New

York, 1960. P. E. Slater and W. G. Bennis, "Democracy Is Inevitable," *Harvard Business Review,* March–April 1964, p. 51. R. Tannenbaum and S. A. David, "Values, Men, and Organizations," *Industrial Management Review,* Winter 1969, vol. 10, pp. 67–83.

2.   F. E. Fiedler, *A Theory of Leadership Effectiveness,* McGraw-Hill, New York, 1967. P. R. Lawrence and J. W. Lorsch, "New Management Job: The Integrator," *Harvard Business Review,* Nov.–Dec. 1967, p. 142.

3.   A. Bavelas, "Communication Patterns in Task-Oriented Groups," *Journal of Acoustical Society of America,* 1950, vol. 22, pp. 725–730. L. S. Christie, R. D. Luce, and J. May, Jr., "Communications and Learning in Task-Oriented Groups," Research Laboratory Electronics, Cambridge, Mass., 1952. H. J. Leavitt, "Some Effects of Certain Communication Patterns on Group Performance," *Journal of Abnormal and Social Psychology,* 1951, vol. 46, pp. 38–50.

4.   H. Guetzkow and W. R. Dill, "Factors in the Organizational Development of Task-Oriented Groups," *Sociometry,* 1957, vol. 20, pp. 175–204. H. Guetzkow and H. A. Simon, "The Impact of Certain Communication Nets Upon Organization and Performance in Task-Oriented Groups," *Management Science,* 1955, vol. 1, pp. 233–250.

5.   M. E. Shaw, G. H. Rothchild, and J. R. Strickland, "Decision Process in Communication Nets," *Journal of Abnormal and Social Psychology,* 1957, vol. 54, pp. 323–330.

6.   A. Bavelas, op. cit.

7.   T. Burns and G. M. Stalker, *Management of Innovation,* Tavistock, London, 1961.

8.   M. B. Miles, "On Temporary Systems," in M. B. Miles, ed., *Innovation in Education,* Columbia University, New York, 1964, pp. 437–492.

9.   J. R. Galbraith, "Matrix Organization Designs," *Business Horizons,* Feb. 1971, pp. 20–40, and *Organization Design,* Addison-Wesley, Reading, Mass., 1977. S. M. Davis and P. R. Lawrence, *Matrix,* Addison-Wesley, Reading, Mass., 1977.

10.   S. A. Davis, "An Organic Problem-Solving Method of Organization Change," *Journal of Applied Behavioral Science,* 1967, no. 3, pp. 3–21.

11.   T. W. Adorno, E. Frenkel-Brunswick, D. J. Levinson, and R. N. Sanford, *The Authoritarian Personality,* Harper, New York, 1950. V. H. Vroom, "Some Personality Determinants of the Effects of Participation," *Journal of Abnormal and Social Psychology,* 1959, vol. 59, pp. 322–327.

CHAPTER 5

1. For an introduction to concepts, analytic methods, and administrative activities that shape marketing management behavior, see P. Kotler, *Marketing Management,* 3d ed., Prentice-Hall, Englewood Cliffs, N.J., 1976; S. H. Britt and H. W. Boyd, Jr., eds., *Marketing Management and Administrative Action,* 4th ed., McGraw-Hill, New York, 1978; D. S. Hopkins, *The Short-Term Marketing Plan,* report no. 565, Conference Board, New York, 1972.

CHAPTER 6

1. See C. W. Churchman, "Managerial Acceptance of Scientific Rec ommendations" *California Management Review,* 1964, vol. 7, pp. 31–38; A. Harvey, "Factors Making for Implementation Success and Failure," *Management Science,* 1970, vol. 16, pp. B312–B320; L. Lonnstedt, "Factors Related to the Implementation of Operations Research Solutions," *Interfaces,* 1975, no. 5, pp. 23–30.

2. Early examples of this approach are illustrated by C. W. Churchman, R. L. Ackoff, and E. L. Arnoff, *Introduction to Operations Research,* Wiley, New York, 1957; J. F. McCloskey and F. N. Trefethen, eds., *Operations Research for Management,* Johns Hopkins University Press, Baltimore, 1956. J. F. McCloskey and J. M. Coppinger, eds., *Operations Research for Management,* vol. 2, Johns Hopkins University Press, Baltimore, 1956.

3. C. J. Grayson, Jr., "Management Science and Business Practice," *Harvard Business Review,* July–August 1973, pp. 41–48. D. G. Malcolm, "On the Need for Improvement in Implementation in O. R.," *Management Science,* 1965, vol. 11, pp. B48–B58. II. N. Shycon, "All Around the Model: Perspectives on MS Applications," *Interfaces,* 1974, no. 4, pp. 21–23.

4. C. W. Churchman and A. H. Schainblatt, "The Researcher and the Manager: A Dialectic of Implementation," *Management Science,* 1965, vol. 11, pp. B69–B87. J. S. Hammond, "The Roles of the Manager and Management Scientist in Successful Implementation," *Sloan Management Review,* 1974, vol. 15, pp. 1–24. J. Huysmans, 'The Effectiveness of the Cognitive-Style Constraint in Implementing Operations Research Proposals," *Management Science,* 1970, vol. 17, pp. 92–104.

5. A. H. Rubenstein, M. Radnor, N. R. Baker, D. R. Heiman, and J. B. McColly, "Some Organizational Factors Related to the Effectiveness

of Management Science Groups in Industry," *Management Science,* vol. 13, pp. B508–B518.

6. Formulated and stated by K. Lewin, "Frontiers in Group Dynamics," *Human Relations,* 1947, vol. 1, pp. 2–38.

7. An early elaboration of the three phases was developed by E. H. Schein, "The Mechanism of Change," in W. Bennis, E. Schein, F. Steele, and D. Berlew, eds., *Interpersonal Dynamics,* Dorsey Press, Homewood, Ill. 1964, pp. 362–378.

8. For a complete description of the research design, the methods, and instruments used to gather data and for statistical analysis of the results see D. E. Zand and R. E. Sorensen, "Theory of Change and the Effective Use of Management Science," *Administrative Science Quarterly,* Dec. 1975, vol. 20, pp. 532–545. R. E. Sorensen and D. E. Zand, "Improving the Implementation of OR/MS Through the Lewin/Schein Model," in R. L. Schultz and D. P. Selvin, eds., *Implementing Operations Research/ Management Science,* American Elsevier, New York, 1975, pp. 217–236.

CHAPTER 7

1. E. P. Learned, C. R. Christensen, K. R. Andrews, and W. D. Guth, *Business Policy: Text and Cases,* R. D. Irwin, Homewood, Ill. 1969. R. L. Katz, *Cases and Concepts in Corporate Strategy,* Prentice-Hall, Englewood Cliffs, N. J., 1970. H. J. Ansoff and R. G. Brandenburg, "The General Manager of the Future," *California Management Review,* Spring 1969, pp. 61–72.

2. Learned et al., op. cit., p. 761.

3. G. W. England, "Personal Value Systems of American Managers," *Academy of Management Journal,* March 1967, pp. 53–68. W. D. Guth and R. Taguiri, "Personal Values and Corporate Strategies," *Harvard Business Review,* Sept.–Oct. 1965, pp. 123–132.

4. C. W. Mills, *The Power Elite,* Oxford University Press, New York, 1956. H. Levinson, *The Exceptional Executive,* Mentor, New York, 1968, p. 120.

5. P. Lorange and R. F. Vancil, "How to Design a Strategic Planning System," *Harvard Business Review,* Sept.–Oct. 1976, pp. 75–81. R. F. Vancil and P. Lorange, "Strategic Planning in Diversified Companies," *Harvard Business Review,* Jan.–Feb. 1975, pp. 81–90.

6. See J. Dewey, *How We Think,* D. C. Heath, New York, 1933; K.

Duncker, "On Problem Solving," *Psychological Monographs,* 1945, vol. 58, no. 270; N. R. F. Maier, *Problem-Solving Discussions and Conferences,* McGraw-Hill, New York, 1963; A. Newell and H. A. Simon, *Human Problem Solving,* Prentice-Hall, Englewood Cliffs, N. J., 1971; H. A. Simon, *The New Science of Management Decision,* Harper, New York, 1960.

7. G. Katona, "Rational Behavior and Economic Behavior," *Psychological Review,* 1953, pp. 309–311.

8. T. C. Sorenson, *Kennedy,* Bantam, New York, 1965, p. 573.

9. T. A. Petit, "Systems Problems of Organizations and Business Policy," *Professional Papers, Division of Business Policy,* Academy of Management, Norman, Okla., 1972.

10. See F J Aguilar, *Scanning the Business Environment,* Macmillan, New York, 1967.

11. C. P. Snow, *Corridors of Power,* Scribner, New York, Macmillan, London and Basingstoke, 1964, pp. 207–208. Reprinted by permission.

12. A. P. Sloan, Jr., *My Years with General Motors,* Macfadden-Bartell, New York, 1965, pp. 179–182.

13. D. A. Saunders, "Twilight of American Woolen," *Fortune,* March 1954, pp. 92–96.

CHAPTER 8

1. For surveys of the composition and structure of boards of directors see J. Bacon, *Corporate Directorship Practices: Membership and Committees of the Board,* report no. 588, Conference Board, New York, 1973. J. Bacon and J. K. Brown, *The Board of Directors: Perspectives and Practices in Nine Countries,* report no. 728, Conference Board, New York, 1977.

2. See P. F. Westbrook, Jr., "The Risks of Serving as a Director," *The Conference Board Record,* July 1974, pp. 55–56; L. Smith, "The Boardroom Is Becoming a Different Scene," *Fortune,* May 8, 1978, pp. 150–170.

3. For example see R. Garrett, Jr., "The SEC Study of Director's Guidelines," *The Conference Board Record,* July 1974, pp. 57–61.

4. For a chronicle of the challenges of being a more effective director see the description of several cases in "End of the Directors' Rubber Stamp: More Risk and Less Willingness to Say Yes," *Business Week,* Sept. 10, 1979, pp. 72–83.

CHAPTER 9

1. For a survey of guides see J. R. Hackman, "Work Design," in J. R. Hackman and J. L. Suttle, eds., *Improving Life at Work,* Goodyear Publishing Co., Santa Monica, Cal., 1977, pp. 96–162. This book has many other informative sections on the management of stability and change. For additional background on guides for organizing stable work see J. R. Hackman and G. R. Oldham, *Work Redesign,* Addison-Wesley, Reading, Mass., 1980.

CHAPTER 10

1. Peter F. Drucker, *The New Society,* Harper, New York, 1950.

2. Ibid., pp. 12–15.

3. Ibid., pp. 13, 14.

4. Ibid., pp. 199, 200.

5. Ibid., p. 3.

6. See Peter F. Drucker, *The Practice of Management,* Harper, New York, 1954, pp. 263–267.

7. Ibid., p. 266.

8. Ibid., pp. 289–299.

9. Ibid., p. 293.

10. Ibid., p. 304.

11. Rensis Likert, *New Patterns of Management,* McGraw-Hill, New York, 1961. Rensis Likert, *The Human Organization,* McGraw-Hill, New York, 1967. F. Herzberg, B. Mausner, and B. Snyderman, *The Motivation to Work,* Wiley, New York, 1959. Victor H. Vroom, *Work and Motivation,* Wiley, New York, 1964. B. M. Bass and J. H. Leavitt, "Experiments in Planning and Operating," *Management Science,* 1963, vol. 9, no. 4, pp. 574–585. B. M. Bass, *Organizational Psychology,* Allyn and Bacon, Boston, 1965. L. W. Porter, E. E. Lawler III, and J. R. Hackman, *Behavior in Organizations,* McGraw-Hill, New York, 1975.

12. Peter F. Drucker, *The Age of Discontinuity,* Harper and Row, New York, 1968, pp. 259–260.

Index